Ad Lib

Bryce Main

Copyrights
Ad Lib
Copyright © 2017 Bryce Main
Cover design by Darren Scott
All Rights Reserved

The characters and events portrayed in this book are entirely fictitious and bear no relation to any events and real persons alive, dead, or in any state as yet to be determined. Any such portrayals are purely coincidental and completely unintended. No part of this book may be reproduced in any form – except by way of quotations or references in articles, reviews, social media sites or blogs – without the written permission of the author.

Dedication

Every book, published either in electronic or printed form, is a journey. The chances are the author will have benefitted from the help and advice of any number of people, directly or indirectly, somewhere along the line.

Ad Lib would not have seen the light of day were it not for the support, encouragement, and copy checking skills of the writer Denise M. Main, the sculptor Shaun Main, the personal trainer and nutritionist Chris Main, and a hundred and one other very talented people who liked what they read before they even saw this book in print.

A large slice of thanks must go to Darren Scott of Truth Design in Manchester, UK. He has a unique facility for taking the very best out of the inside of a book, and transferring that to the outside. The result is a superb cover design that I couldn't be happier with.

A note about spelling: Although I may eventually have readers all over the world, I live in the UK, write in the UK and, therefore, spell in the UK. Any anomalies in the spelling of certain words in Ad Lib may be due to language and cultural differences. They are not necessarily incorrect spellings of the words themselves, and are definitely not meant to cause offence. Have a nice day

Cover concept, design & artwork: Darren Scott of Truth Design

Articles	Page
In the beginning.	8
The guy in the driving seat is very sneaky.	10
Why I still love being in advertising.	12
What's all this creative copywriter malarkey?	14
A great idea doesn't care who it happens to.	16
Great ideas don't amount to a hill of beans.	18
Long live digital...but analogue ain't dead yet.	20
So...you think you're a senior?	22
Everybody needs a hero.	24
I have this love/hate thing going on.	26
Ever thrown your briefs in the bin?	28
I love to see an idea bounce.	30
Why good writers have three thumbs.	32
The Emperor's new website.	34
Whenever I tweet I feel like a twit.	36
So...you're a creative, eh?	38
Scratch my itch.	39
Say...what's the big idea?	41
You're over 50...not over the hill.	43
The TV ad and the hungry wildebeest.	45
I used to have a Comfort Zone.	47
I wanted to be a writer, or The Pope.	49
How long is a piece of string?	51
What's your pet hate?	53
My life is ruled by apples and numbers.	55
A second chance to write your first ad.	57
Deep inside my brain there's a red door.	59
Why I use a Thesaurus.	61
The only rule is there are no rules.	63
Why buy a dog and bark yourself?	65
Now there's a thought.	67
And yet...	69
The best of both worlds.	71
Lonely old man or loveable mog?	74

I need a fix fast.	76
I love Macs.	78
Bill Bernbach is alive...again!	80
I'm old school...and new school.	82
Black Friday punch-ups?	84
Talent never dies.	86
The genie is out of the bottle.	88
Creativity is rearing its beautiful head.	91
Ho...Ho...Ho.	93
Tell them a story.	95
Respect.	97
Punctuated by a ding.	99
Three little words.	101
Want to be a creative? Get a fuzzy brain.	103
There are four kinds of Christmas.	105
Santa and me.	107
I feel a great disturbance in The Force.	109
The birth of advertising...in 300 words.	111
The return of The Spider.	113
Pin back your ears. It's Trotty Time.	116
It's the beginning of the end.	117
Here we go again.	119
Kensitas, creativity, and Jeff Goldblum.	121
Complicated is the new simple.	124
I'm not a Bingeaholic.	127
It could be epic...it might even be mythic.	130
The brain that works differently.	132
Legends, heroes, and dudes.	134
Ozzy Ozbourne worked in a slaughterhouse.	135
May The Force be with you.	137
In the nicest possible way, burger off!	140
The boxer and the street fighter.	142
The old King might be dead.	144
Be a half-decent copywriter in 30 easy steps.	146
Under 30 and over 50 at the same time.	149
Don't sell it to me...make me want to buy it.	151
To block, or not to block? That is the question.	153

If it sounds like ad copy, rewrite it.	155
One plus one equals three...or maybe four.	157
The art of making human noise.	159
You gotta love the big green guy.	161
Open plan or closed door.	163
Always sell the sizzle, never just the sausage.	165
Bezos is no bozo.	168
Remember number 32.	171
I can feel it in my bones.	174
Verbal briefs.	176
Writer's Block? Yeah...right.	178
The importance of not arriving on time.	180
The difference between hearing...and listening.	182
The Theory of Creative Immortality.	184
Passing The Multiple Nose Test.	186
Creativity is contagious...or is it?	188
It takes two to tango.	191
Lightbulb moments.	193
Saving our bacon.	195
On the subject of age and creativity.	197
The night Santa lost his hat.	199
A real pain in the arse.	202
I know a man who knows a man.	204
The woman who thinks she's a chest of drawers.	206
New blood in old veins.	208
Copy supplied by client.	210
When I write my ears don't work.	212
Does my name look big enough in this.	214
Flip sides of the same coin.	216
Why art directors don't snore.	219
The secret life of Comfort Zones.	221
The tools of the trade.	223
Five 'Beetles'.	225
Hearts, souls and Bengal Tigers.	227
The call centre guy named Brandon.	229
Space, privacy, and a kick in the nuts.	232
Don't drop the bloody baton.	235

The coolest damned horse in the race.	238
The day I was saved by a sweetie.	240
The tiger and the goose.	243
Always keep your pitchfork handy.	245
The grumpier you are, the longer you might live.	247
Big ideas, damp squibs, and a bridge too far.	250
Ashes, self-injury, and peanut butter.	253
We've come a long way since Gilgamesh.	255
There are suits...and then there are SUITS!	257
Everything changes, but nothing is truly lost.	259
Mistakes, copy-checkers, and Billy Faulkner.	261
I used to write by the light of the silvery moon.	264
How I discovered the sound of my third voice.	266
Trombones, swooning, and hanging on every word.	268
The best ideas come as jokes.	270
Viv Stanshall, George Orwell, and Apples.	273
You can't use up creativity.	275
Numbers and Letters.	277
Bowstrings, plugs, and Dirty Harry Callahan.	279
Snake oil, rocks, and watershed moments.	281
All the right letters.	283
Advertising, DNA, and the echo of a scream.	286
Punching B. Earl Puckett in the kisser.	288
Leather jackets, eyepatches, and storytelling.	290
Beautiful letters make beautiful words.	293
Nailing my feet to the floor.	296
The Man Who Walked Around The World.	299
The secret life of my little black books.	301
Cerebral volume and The Cocktail Party Effect.	303
Karma's a bitch, Kevin.	305
Ad Lib, Ad Hoc, and throwing balls in the air.	308
References.	309

In the beginning.

In the early hours of August 1st, 1951, a fair amount of yelling and screaming was heard coming from a hospital maternity ward somewhere north of Hadrian's Wall.

It was a Wednesday.

I was introduced to the world in a ceremony that involved lots of gasping and wheezing, having my umbilical cord unwrapped from around my neck, and my face changing from medium blue to bright red.

I've hated blue ever since.

Sixty four years later (give or take), I decided to write a book about some of the stuff that has taken up residence in my grey matter, in the intervening years between then and now. Well...more precisely between the 1980s and now.

Most of it is about advertising and me being (or trying to be) creative. And being a copywriter. Hence the title.

The rest of it is interesting stuff that I used to pack around the advertising bits to hold them in place between my ears. To stop them from going walkabout.

It's definitely, positively, absolutely NOT a "how to" book. I'm not qualified enough for that. I'm not tall enough for that, either. And there are more than enough of those kinds of books around to last a dozen lifetimes.

This is a casual book. A chilled out book. Often off the cuff. Sometimes off the wall. Now and then off the damned reservation.

It's called Ad Lib.

It isn't a novel. It doesn't have a plot. It doesn't have any chapters. But it does have lots of stories.

It's a collection of social media articles, written over the space of a year (or half a lifetime, if you prefer).

Now it's also a book.

This one.

Some of the articles stretch to around three pages. The rest hit the brakes and come to a gentle halt before they fill two.

Perfect for picking up, reading slowly (or quickly) over a nice cup of coffee...or tea...or something stronger. And you never have to worry about losing your place. Because with Ad Lib, your place is wherever you want it to be.

It's the kind of book that makes Advertising feel like the kind of business I'd want to be in, if I wasn't already in it.

It's the kind of book that you'll want to read over and over again. And you don't even need to start at the beginning.

Some people will start at the back, and work their way leisurely to the front.

Others will start somewhere in the middle and stick around for a while. Then go exploring.

Personally, I'd just start wherever you want to, and take it from there.

Forget the destination.

Enjoy the journey...

The guy in the driving seat is very sneaky.

If there's no such thing as predestination, if free will is everything, it's only because that's what the guy in the driving seat wants us to think.

He's very sneaky.

At some point before the age of 15, I realised that I quite liked the idea of playing around with words. At the time, it wasn't as interesting as playing around with girls, but I ended up with fewer slaps across the face.

Girls may have been the great unknown species (still are)...but words led to greater and more unknown worlds.

At some point before the age of 21, I realised that Advertising was one of the worlds I wanted to explore the most.

It took me a while to reach it.

I've been shipwrecked there ever since.

I now have a greater appreciation of the writings of Daniel Defoe.

Over the years, I think I've managed to get the hang of writing passable advertising copy. Occasionally not bad copy. Every now and then bloody good copy.

Then blogs were born and I wrote some of those. Just to flex my muscles, so to speak.

Then the idea of turning blogs into books was born. So I wrote a couple of those.

This is one of them. I hope you like it.

It was written some time between 2015 and 2017. At least that's my story and I'm sticking to it.

In all that time I haven't been able to shake the feeling that every decision I thought I made in life had, in fact, been made for me before I even put in an appearance.

This very book, for instance, was probably predestined; every word, every sentence, being written somewhere in space and time before I even put pen to paper.

This meant I had no say in the matter. I was not to blame.

This was a very reassuring lightbulb moment.

I could write freely, with no blot on my conscience, and no thought of consequences.

However...

The only other feeling I have had over the years that I haven't been able to shake is that predestination might, in fact, be complete bollocks.

Should this prove to be the case, it would mean that I had every say in the matter...and that I definitely was to blame.

With the greatest respect, I plead the fifth.

In fact, just to be safe, I plead them all...

Why I still love being in advertising.

There's a whole stack of reasons why I got into advertising in the first place.

Probably a damned sight more why I stayed in it.

Over the years I've whittled down the number to a just a few. But they're a good few. For the record, here they are:

Because I still enjoy great writing that isn't just in books.

Because I still enjoy great images that exist outside of movies and art galleries.

Because I still get a real buzz out of reading beautifully-written ad copy. Even if it's written by somebody else. No, make that especially if it's written by somebody else.

Because the decision about what makes great ads should still never be made by people only interested in great results.

Because I still think that having a love of words and pictures should be the rule, not merely the exception.

Because I still believe great art directors are artists, not just directors.

Because the best art directors and writers still aspire to be better.

Because I still believe good enough is never good enough.

Because great ideas still don't care who they happen to.

Because quality still matters more than quantity.

Because I still get more of a kick out of making folk happy, rather than merely informing them.

Because I still love the idea of being able to affect the decisions that people make. Even if it's just some of the people. Even if it's just some of the decisions.

Because I still love to help lower the number of clients who decide to buy a dog and bark themselves.

Because I still believe you can't just want to get to the top of the mountain. You have to give a damn how you get there.

Because I've been lucky enough to know plenty of folk who still give a damn.

Because I've been lucky enough to exist on the same planet, at the same time, as some of my advertising heroes.

Because you probably don't even need to look too closely at the copy style of this post to recognise the biggest hero of them all.

I never got to meet any of them.

But I still get to meet their words. And their pictures. And their thinking.

Over...and over...and over again.

That's why...

What's all this creative copywriter malarkey?

Okay. That's it. Enough is enough. There comes a time when you have to draw the line in the sand. Cue sand. Cue big fat line.

What the blue blithering blazes is a creative copywriter?

Is he, or she, some strange hairy beast that has just popped into existence while I was away doing something useful like making coffee?

Watch my lips. Every damned copywriter is, or should be, creative. It goes with the territory. It goes without saying. It comes with the package. You love coming up with ideas? You're creative. You love writing? You're creative. You don't have to be loud. But you better damned well be proud.

And if you don't think you are...go be a plumber.

It doesn't matter whether you're kicking around fun concepts or ploughing your way through reams of technical body copy. It doesn't matter whether your tone of voice is warm and fuzzy or cool and clinical.

It doesn't matter whether you underwrite or overwrite. It doesn't matter whether you use every letter in the alphabet, every word in the thesaurus, every cell in your brain, or just the ones that matter most.

You're creative. Take a bow.

So the next time you feel like putting the word creative in front of the word copywriter...in fact the next time you feel like putting the word copy in front of the word writer...slam on the brakes. Take a deep breath. Grit your teeth. Gird your loins. Stand up and be counted...and tell it like it is.

You're a writer goddamit. You're not creative as an afterthought. You're not creative as an option. You're creative, naturally. Full time. Every time.

It's not just what you do.

It's who you are.

A great idea doesn't care who it happens to.

A great idea doesn't have an ego.

It's not a prima donna. It has no desire to tell the world just how damned clever it is. It doesn't need to bask in any glory. Wallow in any congratulations. Or win any awards. It just needs to sit down at the table before everyone else.

In advertising, great ideas don't just happen to talented creative directors, art directors or copywriters. Although lots of them do.

They don't just happen to suits and creative teams who grind them out with blood, sweat and tears. Although lots of them do.

They don't just happen to folk who have been thinking them up for so long that they've discovered all the short cuts to having them. Although lots of them do.

And they don't just happen to hungry young creative buggers with overactive synapses and underactive experience glands. Although lots of them do.

A great idea doesn't give a baboon's swollen, red backside who it happens to. It has no preferences. No favourites. And certainly no allegiances.

I knew a bricklayer who jumped tracks and went on to become a damned fine copywriter. He had a ton of great ideas. Most of them outdoors while he was building walls.

I've known clients who came up with ideas for Ad campaigns and headlines that more than a few creatives would have strangled their dear old bedridden grandmothers to have had.

I even knew an office cleaner who had the habit of leaning over the shoulders of creatives working late at night and coming up with killer headlines…with no formal training except how to clean up all the shit left behind by folk who couldn't write a killer anything to save their sorry arses.

A great idea doesn't care what sex, size, weight, age, religion, or colour you are. It doesn't care whether coming up with great ideas is your hobby, your job, or your passion.

It just knows it's a great idea. All it really cares about is getting you, and everyone else, to see that.

On their own, great ideas don't amount to a hill of beans.

"Hey, I've got this great idea."
"Really?"
"Yep. It's a real belter."
"A belter, eh?"
"Absolutely. Total winner."
"Oh well done you!"
"Cheers."
"So…whatcha gonna do with this great idea?"
"Eh?"
"What's the plan?"
"Plan?"
"What happens next, stupid?"
"Emm….it's just an idea."
"Aaah…right."

The marvellous thing about great ideas is that absolutely anyone can have one. The terrible thing about them is that absolutely anyone can have one.

Great ideas sit at the heart of all great advertising. Some of them sit at the heart of good advertising. A few of them even sit buried, forgotten, and shrivelled up, at the heart of crap advertising. On their own, great ideas don't amount to a hill of beans. It's what comes after them that makes this business so damned exciting.

All the kicking them around. All the bending them into shape. All the seeing if they've got legs. All the giving them a voice. All the bringing them to life. All the making them printable. All the making them digital. All the making them memorable. Maybe even unforgettable.

And that takes talent, expertise, skill, boldness and bravery. It takes mad men, smart women, communicators and originators. It takes people who think differently and act differently. People who can take the word creativity and do things with it that simply haven't been done before.

It takes suits with loud ties and jeans with loud voices. It takes account directors, handlers, strategists, planners, creative directors, art directors, writers, digital whiz kids...and a million other people.

People who know the business inside out and people who, on glorious occasions, turn the business upside down.

People who know what to do with a great idea.

Long live digital...but analogue ain't dead yet!

Jorian Murray wrote a Linkedin post titled 'Analogue power in 101 words'.

It was one of those short, sweet posts that leave a long, delicious aftertaste in the mouth.

It made me think about the whole digital versus analogue thing.

I'm an old school writer of ad copy (and other stuff) who uses a plethora of new school aids. I started writing ad copy in an age when folk thought words were beautiful. Not merely just necessary to get a message across (and the fewer words used the better).

I've been called a gadget freak. But I have a couple of old manual typewriters. Just to remind myself that sometimes writing in a slower, considered, manner makes me think more about what I commit to paper.

I have a drawer full of analogue writing devices. They don't run on batteries. They run on ink. I hardly ever use them, except to take the odd note. Some more odd than others. As time goes on I've noticed that I use them less and less. I wonder if there will come a time when I don't use them at all. I wonder if there will come a time when my body memory forgets how to form joined-up writing.

I have an analogue timepiece. I like to witness the passage of time rather than just be told about it in an instant.

I love to read printed books, press ads, leaflets, and posters. I prefer them to hang around, keep me company, not disappear and give way to the next piece of fast moving information.

And yet…and yet…I love the idea of powering forward. Pushing ahead. Not getting left behind. Not stagnating. I love websites, emails, social networking, internet access - and the kind of technology that can turn a mobile phone into a device with more computing power than they used to land man on the moon.

So…I feel like opening the nearest window and shouting, 'long live the digital age'.

But I also want to climb up to the nearest rooftop, hang on tight, and yell at the top of my voice, "Analogue is alive and well and still damned kicking. And don't you bloody well forget it."

So...you think you're a senior?

I saw an ad for a senior art director the other day. It said they were looking for someone with at least five years experience.

There was a time when my mouthful of coffee would have ended up over the front of my shirt.

There was a time when my reaction, after I got over the initial stupidity of the timescale, would have been that it was all a big mistake. Surely they meant 10 years. Or 15.

Or longer.

There was a time when five years wouldn't have been long enough for anyone to be called a senior anything. No matter how brilliant and talented they were.

That's only 60 bloody months, for God's sake.

Then I remembered that, for some folk, time can move at a different rate in this game.

I remembered that they can reach a knowledgeable 50 not long after they've hit the ground running at 25.

I remembered that, with a mere five years experience tucked under their belts, they can call themselves senior without fear of being regarded as still slightly damp behind the ears.

There was a time when the title senior was always earned, letter by letter, concept by concept, campaign by campaign, design by design, illustration by illustration, over a damned sight more than just a few years. Not merely stuck on the front of a job description in the blink of an eye like a bloody post-it note.

There was a time when youth and experience were never seen together in the same brain, never mind mentioned in the same breath.

See...I think the phrase "Having a senior moment" has had a bad rap.

I think what it really means is having a brilliant moment. A lightbulb moment. A moment that's the end result of decades of experience.

A sweet moment of aged enlightenment.

One that couldn't be replicated by anyone under 35 if they tried until the cows came home.

One that deserves recognition for being a positive thing to happen...not a negative one.

I like senior moments when they happen to me. I like them when I see them happen to others.

They give us the freedom to do things that we wouldn't normally dream of doing. Like throwing things at folk and swearing at them when they do and say things that piss us off.

Senior moments carry no guilt.

Senior moments are highly creative.

Rant finished.

Another coffee started...

Everybody needs a hero.

Everybody needs a hero.
It doesn't matter what they look like.
It doesn't matter what they sound like.
It doesn't matter how young or old they are.
What matters is that they do stuff…or say stuff…you wish you'd done or said yourself. Or could never even hope of doing or saying in a million bloody years.
What matters is that they possess the kind of talent that can only come from hard graft and integrity, in combination with a sizeable nudge from the big guy upstairs.
What matters is that they're generous enough to share it. And modest enough to make light of it.
I have a hero. His name is David Abbott. He was a giant. He still is.
He's been with me every day of my working life in advertising. And a fair few years before that.
He passed away last year. May 17, 2014. But he's still alive and kicking.
I think about him every time I pick up a pen to write an ad. Every time I switch on the laptop. Every time I think of a headline. Every time I discard 99 out of 100 of them. Every time I put my feet on the desk.
I never met him. Never even got close. Maybe that's how it should be with your heroes.
But I met his work. I became great friends with his words. I became lifelong buddies with his sentences and paragraphs.

Of course he's not the only copywriter whose work I love. But he's the one whose words I can read over…and over…and over again. And enjoy the act just as much the last time as I did the first.

Once or twice, over the years, I've been asked what advice I'd give to anyone who wanted to become a copywriter. I normally laugh. I'm nowhere near competent or knowledgeable enough to offer advice of any kind. But I know a man who is.

In 1995, the D&AD published a book on the art of writing for advertising. It's called The Copy Book. Taschen, the publishers, updated it and it's now on sale through Amazon. It will cost you an arm and probably both legs…but buy it anyway. Or get your agency to buy it.

Amongst all its precious gems is an article written by David Abbott.

Here's just a small taste:

I've never been much of a theoriser about copywriting, but here are five things that I think are more or less true:

Put yourself into your work. Use your life to animate your copy. If something moves you, chances are, it will touch someone else, too.

Think visually. Ask someone to describe a spiral staircase and they'll use their hands as well as words. Sometimes the best copy is no copy.

If you believe that facts persuade (as I do), you'd better learn how to write a list so that it doesn't read like a list.

Confession is good for the soul and for copy, too. Bill Bernbach used to say, "a small admission gains a large acceptance". I still think he was right.

Don't be boring.

Enough said…

I have this love/hate thing going on.

I love open-plan creative departments.
They're noisy. Friendly. Inclusive. Interactive. Expressive. Action-packed. Passionate. Co-operative. Fabulous for instant feedback. Full of life. Full of talent. Full of enthusiasm. Full of ideas. Full of people.
They do exactly what creative departments should do. They create stuff.
Not always the right stuff. And not always great stuff. But a lot of the time what they do is bloody brilliant.
Sometimes, small offices with closed doors are crap for that.
On the other hand…
I hate open-plan creative departments.
They're noisy. Intrusive. Inconvenient and obstructive. They can clog up the personal thought process and shackle the ability to sort the wheat from the chaff between the ears. Exactly what creative departments shouldn't do.
And you can't have a decent fart in them without immediately becoming persona non grata.
The truth is that more often than not, silence is one of the nicest sounds I like to hear outside my head, when I'm being noisy inside it.
Sometimes, small offices with closed doors are great for that.
I suppose I'm a mass of bloody contradictions.
One minute I love wide open spaces…and the next I can't get into a dark, private corner quick enough.
I love to be included in the conversation…but hate to have my thought process interrupted and side-tracked.

Despite what I say out loud, I quietly think that helping to appeal to the hearts and minds of strangers, using an alphabet just 26 letters long, is the dog's bollocks.

Sometimes I can do it when I'm sat in the middle of a cast of thousands. Other times I need to be on the dark side of the moon.

Preferably with lots of coffee.

Ever thrown your briefs in the bin?

I love great briefs.

I love the way they're designed and put together.

I love the way they feel as you run them through your fingers.

I especially love the way the material in them can stretch to cover all the important bits you want covered.

And still have plenty left over to reach the bits you haven't even thought of covering yet.

As my old granny used to say, "better to have it and not need it…than need it and not have it."

Thankfully, throughout my time as a creative, I've been lucky enough to have worked with account handlers, execs, and directors who love great briefs just as much as I do.

Sadly, I've also worked with those who wouldn't recognise or appreciate great briefs if their arses depended on it.

I remember a story told to me a few years back, about a writer who had a pair of shitty, thoughtless briefs plonked on his desk. Monday morning, 9am.

They were thin, crumpled, and colourless. Devoid of any redeeming features.

They hardly covered anything at all…and they had more holes in them than a cheap screen door.

The writer had the hangover from Hell.

He threw the briefs in the bin.

This act was witnessed by the exec who did the plonking. And also by the writer's creative director.

Words were spoken and buttocks clenched. Egos were crushed and headache tablets requested.

The upshot of it all was that the writer fished the briefs out of the bin...then apologised unreservedly for being so unprofessional with his attitude.

The exec fished her reputation out of the toilet...then apologised wholeheartedly for being so unprofessional with her briefs.

Then she supplied him with a new, improved pair of briefs later that same day.

And two days later, he supplied her with campaign copy that was, by all accounts, the pooch's testicles.

It just goes to show.

Even if you start out with shitty briefs and the hangover from Hell, you can still end up with great creative.

I love to see an idea bounce.

Ideas are wonderful, enthusiastic creatures. They're made of rubber and fit nicely in the hand. Writers and art directors, amongst others, love them.

Ideas come into the world bursting with energy and full of possibilities. And they have one goal in mind.

To bounce.

That's how they grow. That's how they learn to talk.

They don't mind what (or who) they bounce off. As long as they come back to the hand they left, a little bit larger, wiser, and happier than they were before.

Walls are always handy as a surface fit for bouncing off.

Doors can never be relied on. Windows...too risky.

The trouble is, walls aren't very clever and, as a rule, don't offer much in the way of growth potential.

Minds are better.

In fact minds are perfect for listening out for an approaching idea. Catching it before it flies by. Bouncing it around. And giving it the chance to show just what it's made of...how creative it can be.

Sadly, not everyone who has an idea, half-decent or brilliant, realises its deep desire to bounce.

They think that by keeping it in their own hands, they're somehow protecting it.

They're wrong.

They think that by not letting it bounce off other creative minds they're keeping it pure and undiluted. Keeping it from becoming sidetracked...twisted...and diminished.

They're all kinds of bloody wrong.

They're keeping it from becoming kicked around. Knocked about. Remembered. Explored. Expanded. Improved. Enjoyed. Hugged. Loved.

An idea that isn't given the chance to bounce simply isn't given the chance to live.

Right. Rant over.

Back to coffee. Black. Strong. Maybe a slice of toast. With a large dollop of crunchy peanut butter.

Now there's an idea…

Why good writers have three thumbs.

There are three rules of thumb when it comes to the physical act of writing.

The first one goes something like this.

Say, for instance, you like to write with a computer. A good a rule of thumb is to try to open your mind and dump the contents down onto the screen. Don't think about it too much. Just do it. Get it all out. Tidy it up later.

It will possibly make you a faster, more productive writer. In theory anyway. But it won't necessarily make you a better one.

The second rule goes something like this.

Say, for example, you like to write with a pen or pencil. A good rule of thumb is to try to take your time and think about what you want to write, before you make a mark on the paper.

It will possibly make you a slower, more considered writer. In theory anyway. But, like the first rule, it won't necessarily make you a better one.

I used to think, many years ago, that the faster I got the words out of my head, the more room I'd have between my ears for other words to take their place. Maybe better words. Maybe better thoughts.

It was always a question of time and space. Helped along by a Remington noiseless manual typewriter. Then, later, by an Amstrad PCW 8256.

Shortly after that, my love affair with Apple Macs started. It never stopped.

Then I discovered that the longer it took to dig the right words out of my head, the less time I needed to spend sorting out the good from the bad. And both of them from the ugly. A process of natural selection was already taking place.

There was just one problem.

The spider.

So this Christmas I'm going to ask The Fat Man In The Red Suit for a new fountain pen. My first in decades. One with interchangeable nibs. I may even go the whole hog and get one that uses bottled ink.

And I'm going to learn how to gussy up my handwriting.

Instead of looking like a drunken spider crawling across the page…it will resemble one that can at least walk in a straight line without falling over.

It might even be able to take a fast corner without feeling dizzy and throwing up.

Of course I'm not sidelining my wonderful MacBook Pro. I'm just going to give it a well-deserved breather every now and then. I might even switch the poor thing off from time to time.

Hopefully, I'll turn from a fast writer into a slower, more thoughtful one. At least some of the time.

I realise my new pen won't turn me into a better writer.

That would be too easy. And too hard.

And as my dear old maternal granny used to say, "If it feels easy, yer no doin' it right, son."

Which brings me to my third rule of thumb. It goes something like this.

Sod the other two thumbs. Just write with your damned heart…

The Emperor's new website.

I came across a website a few months ago that made me want to punch the nearest wall.

It was translated. Into English. By someone whose first language obviously wasn't even a close relative of English.

It may have been a distant cousin. Sadly the distance was too great.

I'm sure it was full of useful information. No doubt compiled by clever, hard-working people. Experts in their field. Or at least highly knowledgeable.

Without doubt it took time to think about, design, and write.

Without doubt it took time to kick around, get feedback from all the right people, and then put live online.

Without doubt it should have been thrown in the trash.

Everyone involved was obviously too scared (or too crap) to tell the powerful client that his nice website wasn't very nice at all.

It was like the dog's bollocks. Only without the dog.

His crusty old advisors had told porky pies. He believed them.

They said it looked great. He said, "Fantastic".

They said it read really well. He said, "Brilliant".

They said it was highly motivational and full of useful information. He said, "Hey...you're the experts. That's good enough for me".

They said a lot and were paid a lot.

Then a small, raggedy-arsed office junior (who secretly happened to be an IT wizard) tapped him on the arm and asked, "Where's your nice new website?"

The powerful client looked down, gasped, and saw the truth. His corporate crown jewels were naked to the world. His company could become a laughing stock.

There was no nice new website. In its place was a website that could have been a thousand times better, if only it had been done properly. More professionally. By the right people.

The powerful client got mad, fired his old Agency and his crusty old advisors on the spot, hired a cracking new Agency, and made the office junior his new head of IT. In charge of all his web presence.

And they all lived happily ever after. Or for quite a few years at least.

Except, of course, for his old Agency and crusty old advisors, who mysteriously disappeared and were never heard of again.

Ever…

Whenever I tweet I feel like a twit.

I'm trying. I really am. I'm a multi-fix-a-day self-confessed social media junkie.

I can post on Facebook and gather up new friends till the cows come home. Occasionally until they go out again. I can cruise Linkedin willy nilly and tickle my profile every five minutes.

But no matter how much I try, I tweet like a twit and can't help thinking that, if I want to say anything meaningful/interesting/hilarious or whatever…I want more than 140 bloody characters. It's probably a character flaw.

My word count is too high. My esteem is too low.

This is not a lesson in brevity. This is not an exercise in compact conversation. This is a tutorial in, "shit, I've run out of bloody tarmac and I haven't even got into second gear".

I know I should suck it up and try harder. I know this is the flash fact relative of flash fiction. I know I should hack it to bloody pieces.

That's not the problem. I'm not even a vegetarian.

I just don't want to tell folk what I had for breakfast. I don't want to announce to the waiting world that I have to go for a pee and I'll be back in five minutes.

I don't want to post a quick sentence or two about what I'm wearing…or where I've been…or where I am…or where I'm going.

I'll leave that up to the gazillions of tweetaholics who seem to do that every day with great delight. God bless them.

Me? I like to ramble. Converse. Expound. Elucidate. Elicit discourse. Give me space. Give me elbow room. Give me land, lots of land, under starry skies above. Don't bloody fence me in.

So I'm going to become a bitly.com guy.

One sentence and a URL-shortened mini-link to a coffee and a leisurely read. Short, medium or long. Simple.

Then I won't feel so much of a twit whenever I tweet.

Now...if only I can stop making a hash of all these damned tag things.

So...you're a creative, eh?

It doesn't matter whether you're old school, or new school. Whether you're a wizard with the words or magic with a marker.

It doesn't matter whether you're analogue or digital. Whether you're online, offline, in line, out of line, or way over the line.

It doesn't matter whether you're lightweight, heavyweight, dead weight, or worth your weight in bloody gold. Whether you're full of awards, full of bright ideas or just plain full of shit.

It doesn't matter whether you're on the way in, on the way out, on the way up or on the way down. Whether you clam up when you have to talk the talk, or step up to be counted when you have to walk the walk.

It doesn't matter whether you're the best damned thing since sliced bread, or your own worst enemy. Whether you work 9 to 5 and bugger off, or you stay on the job 24/7 until the job gets done.

It doesn't matter whether you're short haired, long haired, grey haired or no bloody haired at all. Whether your brain is the size of a planet, or your opinion of yourself is as big as Alaska.

It doesn't matter whether you're lived-in, burned-out, screwed-up, or broken- down. Whether you're overlooked, overbooked, underpaid, or underappreciated.

It doesn't matter whether you're a joy to behold, or a real pain in the arse. Whether you're a laugh a minute, or as serious as a heart attack.

The only thing that matters is the length of the gap.

The one between the moment you get asked why you're a creative...and the moment you remember the answer.

Scratch my itch.

I hate dumb, pushy advertising. Always have. Always will.

I hate the idea of being strong-armed into spending money I really don't have, to buy something I really don't need, from someone who really has no interest in me whatsoever.

I love clever, inspired advertising. Always have. Always will.

I love the kind that introduces itself politely. The kind that intrigues me. Entertains me. Informs me. Excites me. Wants to get to know me. Appeals to my intellect. My sense of humour. Scratches my itch. Tells me secrets. Puts me at ease. Helps me to make up my own mind.

I hate the kind that calls me up at home at eight at night, in a foreign accent, pretending to be someone with an English name, promising they're not trying to sell me anything.

I hate the kind that makes me feel that I'm being scammed, flim-flammed, taken for a ride, taken for a fool.

The kind that tries to con me into spending time with them in the hope that, somewhere down the line, I'll spend money with them.

Watch my lips.

I'll decide what I want to buy. I'll decide when I'm ready to buy. And I'll decide who I want to buy from.

At least that's my story…and I'm bloody well sticking to it.

For God-knows how many years, it seems like the worst kind of marketing has been fighting to squeeze itself into the driving seat…and it doesn't give a shit who it shoves out the car door.

It doesn't have any scruples. Doesn't have any morals. Doesn't have a shred of decency. And it sure as Hell doesn't have any goddam truth or honesty.

This business has enough folk who don't give a tinker's cuss about anyone except themselves. All they want is my time and as much of my money as they can get – as quickly as they can get it – before locking up shop and galloping out of town on the fastest horse in the stable.

Sod them. They can't scratch my itch.

Thankfully, this business also has more than enough of the other kind of folk. The clever ones. The genuine ones.

The ones who do give a tinker's cuss. Who do have morals, decency, honesty, style…and real bloody talent.

They're the ones who don't leave a sour taste in my mouth. They're the ones who don't make my palms sweat.

They're the ones ready, willing, and able to have a damned good bare-knuckle punch-up, if necessary, to stay in the driving seat. They know what they're doing. They know why they're doing it.

They know where I want to go and they want to come with me.

They don't want to sell me anything. They just want to help me buy something. Big difference.

They can scratch my itch.

Say...what's the big idea?

I had a big idea last night.

It happened about half an hour after I went to bed. Not long after that I was half asleep. Drifting along in that limbo land where experts say lots of creative thinking takes place. Salvador Dali was a bugger for that.

Mind you, he was a bugger for a lot of weird shit. Bless him.

Anyway, I can't remember the exact details of my big idea. In fact I can't remember anything about it at all. Just that I had it...and I had a strong feeling that it was, as my sister in Glasgow would say, a real stoater!

I did remember thinking at the time that it would be a damned good idea to sit up in bed, grab my notebook from the bedside cabinet, and scribble my big idea down.

Just a few key words and phrases. Maybe a paragraph or two. So when I woke up in the morning, it would wake up with me.

But instead, I turned over and travelled the rest of the way uninterrupted into the land of nod.

I woke up at 7am sharp. My big idea didn't.

As far as I know it's still fast asleep. Floating around in the space between my ears.

But, somewhere along the way, it must have bumped into the part of my brain that stores my memories.

One came loose.

An agency I worked at, many moons ago, had a senior writer who had a habit of dozing off in one of the large leather sofas in the creative department.

At the time, I thought he was just knackered from the quantity of body copy he wrote. Or said he wrote. Or possibly he was recovering from the quantity of wine consumed the night before. Or said he consumed. Or maybe he was just bloody lazy.

Now, looking back, I realise that he was in limbo. Shifting furniture around behind his eyes. Making space for his big ideas to put in an appearance.

And that got me thinking.

If more creative departments in more agencies had more sofas where more people could have more limbo-like snoozes…then maybe more folk would have more big ideas.

The problem, of course, would be waking up in time to do the scribbling bit, before the falling asleep bit kicked in.

Maybe I've found a small part of my big idea.

I just need to lay down on this sofa for five minutes, and try to figure out where the rest of it is…

You're over 50...not over the hill.

There was a time when I used to merely like B&Q. Then, years ago, I came to really, really like them.

They did something that made them go up a notch or ten in my estimation. They listened to their customers.

Or rather, they listened to their customers' complaints.

They complained that when they came into the store and asked the nearest whippersnapper about the interior dimensions of plastic piping…or the best exterior varnish…or any one of a thousand other questions, said whippersnapper tended to grunt, scratch their head, and display a level of knowledge that proved decisively they didn't have a bloody clue.

They were good at filling shelves, pointing to the right aisle, carrying stuff, and looking busy. They were also good at asking someone else.

So the clever folk at B&Q started employing more people who did have a bloody clue. Or at least looked like they did. And sounded like they did.

Invariably these people were older, some near retirement, grey haired, sometimes blue rinsed…and knowledgeable in many things nuts, bolts and DIY.

Just when they thought they were over the hill and unemployable, they were delighted to find themselves useful again. And employed.

And they were more than willing to pass on decades of knowledge (and common sense) to customers who were tickled pink that B&Q actually cared about them again.

It was a masterstroke.

The other day I saw a Linkedin post from someone asking if she was too old to get a copywriting job in an ad agency. She was a mere 56.

My first thought was to shout "bollocks!" out loud. My second thought was to belay the first thought and swallow my mouthful of coffee.

I know that advertising is dominated by young people. It's a business that thrives on energy and ideas. Energy expended and ideas generated by lots of young, talented creatives. With gym memberships and no grey hair.

But it's also a business that thrives on knowledge and experience...and these always takes time to accumulate. And time is something that folk over 50 have been chalking up for decades.

There must be a whole stack of agencies and clients who would love to work with enthusiastic creatives who are full of ideas, despite being full of years.

It doesn't matter whether they're staffers or freelancers. It doesn't matter whether their grown-up kids call them mum or dad. And it sure as Hell doesn't matter how grey their grey cells are.

The only thing that matters is that people who can do a great job get together with people who need a great job done.

It's not rocket science. It's not brain surgery.

It's creativity.

And creativity doesn't give a damn who it happens to. Or when they were born.

The TV ad and the hungry wildebeest.

I remember a time when there were no ads on the telly.

Programmes got watched all the way through and interruptions were unheard of.

If you wanted a cuppa, you either bloody well waited or you missed something. Usually something important.

Sod's law.

Then there was a time when ads on the telly were everywhere (except the BBC, of course).

Ad agencies and their clients rubbed their hands in glee at the prospect of captive audiences and increased sales.

Then there was a time when remote controls came in and made it a doddle to switch channels from the comfort of the armchair.

You didn't have to press any buttons on the telly at the other end of the room. You just let your fingers do the walking.

If you didn't like the ads, you switched channels for a few minutes, watched a scrawny lion pull down a fully grown wildebeest, and switched back before the gory bit.

Or you used the commercial break to nip through to the kitchen and make a cuppa. Possibly even a sandwich.

Now, with Sky and Virgin and Netflix and God knows whatever else, you can do the following:

One: Fast-forward over the (mostly) crap ads on telly and pretend they never existed.

Two: PAUSE the action when the programme's about to start up again.

Three: Make a cuppa.

Four: Nip to the loo.

Five: Nip to the grocery store.
Six: Decorate the bedroom.
Seven: Go on holiday.

I remember watching a nature programme when I switched channels a few years back. It was about the annual Great Migration of about 1.5 million Wildebeest and about 300,000 Zebra in East Africa.

The principle went something like this.

You're a hungry wildebeest. With children. You eat your fill of grass until there's nothing left to eat, then you move on until you find somewhere else with lots to eat.

You come across many hurdles. Some of them with large teeth. But you persevere.

You keep on doing this until, eventually, you come back to where you started.

Then you do it all over again. Every year.

It got me thinking.

Whether advertising diminishes on the telly and grows somewhere else online…whether new ways of catching consumers' attention are created and new ways of helping them part with their money are developed…it doesn't matter.

It all comes down to this.

Wildebeest and zebra (and hungry lions) need to eat. Need to survive and prosper.

And hungry consumers need to buy. Need to survive and prosper.

It doesn't matter how far they have to go to do it. And it doesn't matter how easy it is to do, or how many obstacles they have to overcome.

It only matters that they know what they need. And they know where to go to get it.

Every time they need it.

That's where we come in…

I used to have a Comfort Zone.

I used to have a creative bubble. It wasn't very big.

I used to have a Comfort Zone, too.

It was inside my bubble, and it was warm and cuddly and very protective.

It made me feel cared for. Approved of. I could write copy about things I knew about.

Really knew about.

I knew my limitations and so did my Comfort Zone.

My creative bubble was intact. In good nick. Unmolested.

I remember having a conversation with an agency director who said they came across a nice piece of copy and knew instantly that I had written it.

At the time, he made me feel that my copy had a voice and the voice was unique. Life was good.

Every time I wrote something it felt like I was getting back together with an old friend.

Then, some time later, I had another conversation with the same director. This time he wasn't so complimentary.

He said my copy was getting safe. Predictable. Unadventurous. Boring.

I explained that I was in my comfort zone when I wrote it. He said that much was obvious.

I explained that I was surrounded by my creative bubble at the time. He said that it was about time somebody burst the bloody thing.

I explained that the words came out faster when I was writing about something I was familiar with.

He said that maybe they'd come out better if I slowed down. Or wrote about something I knew bugger all about.

So I did.

And that's when I discovered my Uncomfort Zone.

It doesn't have a creative bubble surrounding it. In fact it doesn't have any bloody bubble.

It's completely open to the world.

It can go where it wants. Try what it wants. Say what it wants.

With it I can write copy that's short, fat and hairy…or long, slim and smooth.

With it, I can be serious, funny, straight, flexible, friendly, professional, knowledgeable, brave, fascinating, right on the button or completely off the wall.

With it I can start out knowing nothing at all…and end up finding out something that nobody else knew.

I can be less predictable. More persuasive. More ready to ignore the bullshit. More willing to say what needs to be said. More able to write what needs to be written.

Less of a pain in the arse. Sometimes.

A colleague said he didn't like my new Uncomfort Zone.

He said it made him feel uncomfortable.

I told him to go to Hell.

I'm still working on being more tactful…

When I was young, I wanted to be a writer, or The Pope.

When I was a kid I wanted to revel in the beauty of words or wear white and have millions bow down before me.

It really was an either-or thing. I was a ten year old kid with ears like jug handles and a healthy sense of Catholic guilt. What the Hell did I know?

The Pope thing only lasted until they stopped saying the mass in Latin, and I realised that everything had become lost in translation and incense.

But the beauty of words has lasted a lifetime. So far.

One way or another.

I dreamed of becoming a famous novelist and filling hearts and minds with memorable stories.

Instead, I became an average copywriter and tried to empty wallets of hard-earned cash. I tried my best.

Often, my best wasn't even near good enough.

Due to my sterling efforts, many would-be consumers ended up with more money in their wallets than they might otherwise have done, had I been better at my job.

In my defence, I began writing at a time when there existed in this business, copywriters (men and women) with more talent in their little fingers than I and all my ancestors had in every one of our collective digits.

That was then. This is now.

Today my writing has improved. My practice hasn't made me perfect. Not even close. But at least it has made me better.

But the quality and quantity of great copywriters around these days seems to have diminished.

A love of words seems to have been shoved onto the back burner. Its place looks to have been taken by a love of creating as many ways as possible to interrupt the lives of consumers, every minute of the damned day and night.

A dangerous tactic.

Consumers love stories. We love emotion. We love heroes. Villains. Hope. Fun. Life in all its glorious (and sometimes terrible) beauty. We love touchy feely. We love itchy scratchy.

We love things that affect our hearts. Not just our heads.

We love to experience words worth reading. Not just worth writing.

We don't always love fast. Sometimes we love slow.

And we don't like being interrupted.

I can't help but think that, sooner or later, all those damned interruptions will, themselves, be interrupted.

In fact it's happening already.

The global rise of ad blocking is a case in point.

Maybe the love of words is coming off the back burner.

Maybe we're finally turning the heat back up on the kind of copy, with the kind of stories, that reach consumers' hearts as well as their wallets.

I wonder what kind of books The Pope reads.

Apart from the obvious…

How long is a piece of string?

I remember when I used to have lots of thinking time.
I remember when I could rely on writing copy one day, giving it the overnight test, and seeing whether it passed the test the next day.
Or not.
Occasionally, if I was lucky, overnight lasted a whole weekend. Or longer.
It still happens. Just not as much.
The desire to want solutions yesterday is at odds with the need to expend grey cells trying to get the best solution possible.
A quick answer is, unfortunately, often more acceptable than a right one.
It pisses me off no end.
On the other hand, I remember giving myself a whole hour to come up with a cracking headline…and having a lightbulb moment within the first five minutes.
I remember sitting down in a quiet room with an art director for days and covering the walls with ideas. Then realising that the first idea we came up with was the best one we had.
I also remember needing a slice of inspiration instantly. Right now. And I came up with a great thought when my back was against the wall, my pulse was racing, and I had nowhere to run.
Or hide.
Creative departments are full of pieces of string of indeterminate lengths.
Creative briefs are often full of restrictions.

And they don't always like each other.

Out of this recipe for a punch-up, however, comes magic.

A case in point…

The time was the early 1970's. The agency was CDP. The copywriter was Terry Lovelock. The product was Heineken lager.

For eight weeks, or so the story goes, Lovelock and his art director Vernon Howe tried to come up with a killer idea.

They came up with nada. Zero. Zilch. Zippo.

Finally, Lovelock fled to Marrakesh, with the words of his legendary agency head, Frank Lowe, ringing in his ears.

"Come back with a campaign, or don't come back at all."

There, he awoke early one morning around 3, grabbed a pen and wrote the following line:

"Heineken refreshes the parts other beers cannot reach".

The rest, as they say, is history.

The truth is, it doesn't matter how short or how long your piece of string is.

It doesn't matter whether you're sat doodling in a comfy chair, in a nice creative department, in a nice creative agency. Or whether you bugger off in a panic to a bolthole a million miles away.

Your brilliant idea will turn the tables.

It will hunt you down.

And it will find you…

What's your pet hate?

I have a pet hate.
Well, truth be told, I have a few. But one stands head and shoulders above the rest.
I hate creatives taking the credit for other creatives' work.
It doesn't matter how brilliant or crap the work is.
It doesn't matter whether it's words or images.
It doesn't matter whether it's the germ of an idea, or a whole damned multimedia campaign.
It doesn't matter if you saw it accidentally over someone else's shoulder.
It doesn't matter if you like it so much that you'd tear someone's arm off and beat them to death with the soggy end, just to put your name on it.
If it's not yours…keep your damned mitts off it.
Over the years I've seen it happen time and time again. Sometimes behind closed doors. Other times blatantly and right in front of the poor sod who was too hurt, too shocked, or too timid to stand up for themselves.
Ownership doesn't belong to the one with the loudest mouth. It doesn't belong to the one with the longest service record. It doesn't belong to the one with the biggest salary. And it sure as dammit doesn't belong to the ones trying to feed their own damned egos while others go hungry.
It belongs to the one (or more) whose imagination brought the work kicking and screaming into the world.

It belongs to the one (or more) who expended a shit load of blood, sweat and tears to create something that gave them goosebumps over every square inch of their skin…and everywhere underneath it.

Nobody else owns it except them.

Nobody else deserves the credit except them.

Ever.

There's a special place in Hell reserved for those who claim the credit that other folk rightly deserve.

There are people there waiting to welcome them.

They have baseball bats…

My life is ruled by apples and numbers.

I have a MacBook Pro. An iPad 2. A classic iPod 160GB. And the very latest iPhone 6 (yep, the big one).

I also have drawers full of pencils and pens. Reams of paper. And two very cool manual typewriters. One of them is a light blue Lettera 32 Olivetti. Same model as Cormac McCarthy's. The one that sold for $254,500 at auction, at Christies, in 2009.

Mine doesn't write as well as his.

Compared to mine, his is a filthy rich giant in a world of portable literary output.

Compared to his, mine is a poor, talentless smear, spread over the surface of an underused return key

I used to harbour secret feelings of admiration.

Then I harboured secret feelings of jealousy.

After that I harboured secret feelings of resentment.

Recently I heard about other laptops, tablets and mobiles that were better writers than mine. Smarter. More supportive.

Then a penny dropped.

My tools were not on my side. They didn't have my back. They weren't being up front with me. They were undermining my potential. They weren't giving me their best efforts. They had ulterior motives.

Around about this time, I began to get a strange feeling between my ears.

It started as a tingle. Grew into a throb. Then into a full-blown barrage of wallops and thumps.

The kind you hear when someone's slamming a clenched fist repeatedly against a locked door, trying to get attention. Trying to get in. Or out.

Then I heard a voice.

It had a Scottish accent. Very like mine. In fact exactly like mine.

It was yelling about being locked up. Being kept in the shadows. Not being listened to. Not being in control. Being subservient to electronic stuff too clever for its own damned good.

It was highly pissed off.

Then I had a lightbulb moment. It may have lasted longer.

I realised that, when it came to writing, all the tools in the world didn't amount to a hill of beans, apart from one. The grey one that fitted nicely in the space between my ears.

And it didn't need any damned tech at all.

Well, not at the beginning.

Maybe I could go no-tech and write all my first drafts in pencil.

It's said that Steinbeck used 300 of them to write East of Eden.

Shit…that's almost a large tree branch and a bucket full of graphite.

And I bet each one of his pencils was a damned sight more talented and supportive than each one of mine.

Bugger…

A second chance to write your first ad.

I can remember the first ad I ever wrote.
I can remember it as if I'd written it this morning.
I wrote it 30 years ago.
It was only a simple press ad. A small ad. It should have been a big deal.
It was for a gas-powered radio.
I thought the account exec was taking the piss.
This was my first ad dammit. This wasn't a trial run.
I felt let down. I wanted more of a landmark. I wrote it in half an hour. Start to finish. I was cocksure. I was confident. I was stupid.
Once it was done it was done. There was no going back. There were no rewrites. No rethinks. No second chances. No overnight test. This was it.
I was no longer a copy virgin.
I was something else entirely. Apart from a prat.
Like a newborn duckling, my ad imprinted itself on the first thing it saw at birth.
Me.
I became mama.
In that moment, the true value of firsts was hammered home.
My first kiss. My first love. The first time I got dumped. My first agency. The first time I wrote a headline I loved. The first time my headline got dumped.
They were all my ducklings.
And they're still following me around to this day.
It made me think.

I'm going to hunt out my little gas-powered radio press ad. It's in a dusty folder somewhere in the attic.

I'm going to take a long, hard look at it.

Then I'm going to re-write it.

Not because I think I can write it better, which undoubtedly I can.

Not because after 30 years gas and radio technology have moved on and it needs updating, which undoubtedly it does.

But because I think it deserves a shot at being a better first ad.

Even if it is second time around.

Wild ducks, on average, live longer than those in captivity.

The world record is held by a Mallard drake that lived to the ripe old age of 27.

That's not far short of my time in the business.

There's no record of any duckling, beautiful or ugly, growing up in wild or captured obscurity, dying, being resurrected (perfectly preserved) and given another chance at life.

Well, now there is.

I think I'll name him Lazarus.

Or Bob...

Deep inside my brain there's a red door.

Deep inside my brain there are lots of doors. One of them is red.

Behind it, there's a dark room.

Inside the room, covering one of the walls, there's a large bank of TV screens.

They're always on.

In front of the screens there's a long line of desks and chairs.

On the desks are large red buttons.

On the chairs are small, nervous men.

On the screens is a perfect storm of marketing images and messages. All trying to sell me something. Tell me something. Get me to do something. Go somewhere. Say something. Think something.

Now.

The job of the small, nervous men is to press their red buttons each time they see something on the screens they think might interest me.

They need fast reactions, because the images and the messages don't hang around for long.

But they can't press their buttons too soon or too often, because although I can probably see thousands of images and messages in any given day…the number I actually notice is only in the hundreds.

The very, very low hundreds.

And the number I actually react to is even less.

So the small, nervous men have to be very careful. Because each time they screw up and show me something I'm not interested in, they get hauled away, kicking and screaming, never to be seen again.

It's not a pretty sight.

I can't help thinking there must be a better, less painful, more successful way for me to get the clever marketing messages I want to see and hear, without having to put up with all the crap ones I don't.

Deep inside my brain there's a green door...

Why I use a Thesaurus.

"Hello. My name's Bryce, and I'm a Thesauraholic…"

Some say the famed Thesaurus is the book that good copywriters are supposed to steer clear of. Avoid like the plague. Have no truck with.

Watch my lips.

Bollocks!

I have a well-thumbed copy of Roget's International, 7th Edition, on my desk. It's very handy.

But not for the reason you might think.

I don't use it to hunt for alternatives to avoid repetition. I don't use it to search for synonyms to steer clear of reiteration. And I tend to give antonyms a wide berth. Well…not always.

Mostly, I use my Roget's to fill gaps. Apertures. Openings. Spaces. Cavities. Fissures. Even orifices, on memorable occasions.

I have what some might call Leaky Memory Syndrome.

It's a little like Leaky Gut Syndrome. But not a lot.

My brain has little perforations, much like a tea bag, where appropriate words and phrases have a habit of squeezing through and disappearing out the nearest apertures.

Or any apertures.

I suspect I'm not the only one who suffers from it. I have a sneaky feeling that there are other writers who endure the agonising effects of Leaky Memory Syndrome.

Generally it attacks the more intelligent ones. The ones with too much information between their ears and not enough room to store it all. The ones who know so many words that fighting for space commonly leads to outbreaks of violence and extremely bad behaviour in the limbic system.

This, in turn, leads to a desire felt by many words to escape. Do a runner. Fly the coop. Skedaddle. Vamoose.

Sometimes too many make a break for it, which leaves lots of empty spaces. A surfeit, you might say.

Spaces that need to be filled.

Cue my Roget's International thingy.

When I feel an attack of Leaky whatsit coming on, I pick up my doohickey, open it anywhere…and simply read.

I also regularly self-medicate. Usually five minutes twice a day, morning and evening, does the trick to top up the old grey thingamabob.

I'm sure there's an equivalent for art directors.

I just can't remember what it is…

The only rule is there are no rules.

For some folk advertising is about following the rules.

It's about in with the new always following out with the old.

It's about middle-aged folk with too many memories and too much grey hair having no damned energy and thinking they know everything.

It's about young blood, hungry to learn, having too much energy and not being scared of anything.

It's about giving birth to big ideas and not stopping working on them till they grow into big campaigns. Changing minds. Changing buying habits.

It's about somebody doing the words. Somebody else doing the pictures. Joining them together. And thinking there isn't a bigger buzz in the known universe.

Then there are other folk who think that advertising is about breaking the rules.

Clients are writers, art directors are writers, writers are art directors, everyone does concepts, the bottom line rules the top line, and digital is the new analogue. Macs are gods, technology is talent, big data is big news, and loyalty is something your dog gives you when you get home from the agency at 2.am.

Some folk remember what they were doing when Kennedy was shot and man landed on the moon.

I remember the moment game-changers called Millennials rode into town…and the only rule left in advertising was that there were no damned rules.

They're not just engaged with digital technology…they're bloody married to it.

Hard wired into the brain. Bless their 18-33 year old cotton socks.

According to a recent study, nearly 40 per cent of them feel that they're missing something if they're not on Facebook or Twitter every day. They're probably also on Linkedin, Flickr, Snapshot, Instagram, Pinterest, and a whole bucketload of other social network platforms.

As consumers they're also, apparently, moving away from advertising as a trusted source of brand advice. Try that one out for a holy shit moment.

They're acting in new ways. Thinking in new ways. They now make up 44 per cent of the workforce in advertising. They don't give a damn about history. And they're reshaping the industry.

They're more collaborative…more socially conscious…less insular…more democratic…more exciting…and they scare the shit out of all those still hanging on with broken nails to the way things used to be done.

They're frank. Fearless. Versatile. Valuable. Direct. Loud. And proud. They have itchy feet. Itchy fingers. And itchy minds.

They're free-flowing liquid talent, more in touch with leading edge media…and more in tune than anyone else under forty with the way consumers think and act.

They're a new broom. A breath of fresh air. A seismic shift. And, some would say, the best thing to hit advertising since somebody holding a sharp knife looked at an unsliced loaf and had a lightbulb moment.

Exactly the kind of folk I came into this business 30 years ago to work with…

Why buy a dog and bark yourself?

I never saw the point of buying a dog and barking myself.

Then I had a conversation about words with an overweight, vertically challenged marketing director.

He loved them.

Words...not dogs.

In fact he adored them.

Not just the way they looked. Not just their shape. For as long as he could remember he loved the sounds they made when they whizzed around in his head.

Or came out of his mouth.

In fact he loved them so much he took a special interest in the words used by the writers in his company's ad agency. Particularly the words used by the writers working on his account. Writing about his products.

He loved those words best of all.

Especially as many of them were his.

It was a source of great pride to him that he could put his own thumbprint on the copy and images sent to him by the agency for approval.

Sometimes he didn't stop with his thumbs.

He spent many long hours pouring over Style. Content. Rhythm. Syntax. Structure. Balance. Tone of voice. Texture. Colour. Photography. Typography.

The agency spent many long hours trying to figure out how to tell him politely but firmly to butt out and let them do their job.

They, after all, didn't try to tell him how to do his.

The people in the creative department weren't so polite.

In fact they were bloody pissed off.

They didn't like working on his account. They didn't like having their copy altered. They didn't like having their visuals altered. They didn't like having their thinking altered.

They didn't like him. He didn't like them.

Then one of their campaigns…one of his campaigns…won an award. A big one. An important one.

A creative one.

Naturally the CD and creative team had a great time at the award ceremony. They stayed in a posh hotel. Ate too much food. Drank too much alcohol.

They didn't invite the overweight, vertically challenged Marketing Director to join them.

Naturally the agency was fired a week later.

The small client took his big business to another agency.

A better one. A cleverer one.

One that appreciated his input and recognised his love of creativity.

They quite enjoyed his barking, too. It showed he cared. It kept them on their toes.

They loved his intelligence. They loved his passion.

And they really loved his budgets…

Now there's a thought.

Thanks to Dr. Travis Bradberry (via Raj S. Randhawa on Linkedin), for letting me know that the average person has 70,000 thoughts each day. [1]

It got me thinking.

I wonder if that includes any thoughts I might have after midnight while I'm fast asleep.

Does my brain use this downtime to chill out? Or does it decide that, since my body is recumbent and immobile, it has more diverted energy that can be used to ramp up my thought process?

And another thing.

Do creative folk have more thoughts than uncreative folk in any given day? And if so, does that mean that the average day in the average creative department is full of folk who crack the 100,000 thought mark?

And do really, REALLY creative folk get anywhere near the 200,000 mark? In fact…is there even ROOM for 200,000 thoughts in any brain in the space of 24 hours?

Could the rest of our bodies even function while our brains are operating at that rate?

And what about organising all those thoughts?

Included in the excellent post I mentioned above is this thought-provoking fact. In a recent study conducted at the National Institute on Aging, it was found that a disorganised mind is bad for you.

Who knew!

Apparently it can lead to stress, negativity, and impulsivity. Plus weight gain, heart disease, sleep problems, and migraines.

It can also lead to a distinct drop in humour levels.

I think that's the most worrying side-effect of them all.

Upwards of a hundred thousand thoughts a day and not one of them worth a titter? Now that scares the bejazus out of me.

Perversely, it does give me some sort of comfort.

I like a large splattering of humour in my mental diet.

My daily thought count must, therefore, be on the lower side. Say between 50,000 and 100,000, or thereabouts.

In fact just writing this probably got rid of around 5,000 of them. Give or take.

Maybe my brain simply doesn't have enough storage to hold the staggering amount of thoughts that separate me from my larger brained peers.

On the other hand, maybe brains are an in-and-out sort of thing.

Space between the ears is, after all, limited.

You only keep the good thoughts. The rest get dumped to make room.

And maybe you don't need to have all those good thoughts at your fingertips.

Maybe you just need the really important ones on the front desk, and the rest somewhere tucked away safely in a locked filing cabinet in the back office until they're needed. Or until tomorrow, when a new lot of thoughts come in.

Just don't lose the key…

And yet...

I love advertising. I've loved it from the moment I became aware of it. From the moment it became aware of me.

I love its intelligence. Its creativity. Its style. Its power of persuasion. I love its ability to make me laugh. Make me think. Make me stop. Make me act. Make me shed a few pounds. Sometimes even make me shed a few tears.

I love its refusal to stand still. Its fearlessness. Its bravery. Its predictability. Its ability to do something completely unexpected. Its determination to give me what I want...when I want it...where I want it...and for the price I want. Or less.

I love it for showing me the world. Showing me the past, present and future. Showing me what's possible. Showing me that when folk tell me things are impossible they're probably not trying hard enough.

I love it for the buzz. The thrill. The blank slate. The hundred answers to a single question. The hundred solutions to a single problem.

I love it for the people. The hearts. The minds. The dreams and aspirations. The wonderful trees that bear strange fruit. The wonderful fruits that bear strange tastes.

And yet...

I hate advertising. I've hated it from the moment I became aware that sometimes it bends the truth. Sometimes it's not completely honest, legal and decent. Sometimes it makes me feel uncomfortable and not in a good way.

I hate the way it can manipulate the thoughts and actions of people who don't even see it happening. Don't even see it coming. And smile while it's doing it.

I hate it for the way it takes talent and burns it up. The way it takes great ideas and tones them down. The way it shouts at you from every direction at once. The way it stays quiet when it should be shouting from the rooftops.

And yet…

I love advertising. I love the way it starts from nothing and ends up with everything that means anything. I love the way it bends some rules, breaks others, and leaves the rest alone.

I love the thoughts it puts between our ears that help to make this business one that's always trying to be better than it used to be.

I love the breath of fresh air it brings to a product or service that's lived its life in a locked room with no windows.

I love the way it can tear down walls and build up futures. Push up expectations and knock over negative obstacles without a single thought for the consequences.

I love the way it makes life easier, better, more enjoyable…and more liveable.

All with a simple image.

And a few well-chosen words…

The best of both worlds.

Imagine…

There are two very large towns within spitting distance of each other.

Town A, (lots of phlegm…lots of sitting down) has Sky TV, internet, satellite reception, email, phone, texting, four newspapers, a website, and social networking, all up the wazoo. It moves its fingers and eyes to the beat of the modern digital age.

The town's businesses have a combined annual advertising budget of a gazillion squideroons. It allows those in charge to reach everyone in the surrounding area and shove their marketing messages down the throats of all the inhabitants. Large or small. Rich or poor. Twenty-four-seven.

They're very progressive.

They love change. In fact the more change the better. Can't get enough of it.

They communicate with the world, and the world is only too happy to communicate back. Well, some of it.

But there are those in Town A who secretly love the idea of keeping things exactly as they are.

Then there's Town B, (not a lot of phlegm…lots of natural cardio).

It doesn't have any amazing technological stuff. In their wisdom, the town elders have decided that nearby Town A is run by The Devil and all Town B needs to communicate with itself is one cheap weekly newspaper. Thirty per cent of which is made up of adverts. And the only content the adverts are allowed is factual.

No fancy stuff. No pretty pictures. No clever writing. Just the facts, ma'am.

The combined marketing budget of Town B's businesses wouldn't cover a skinny gnat's arse.

The town elders believe that anyone who really wants to sell anything to anyone else can't be trusted with the truth. And the truth is that anyone who wants to buy anything shouldn't get it until they really need it. All those damned sales folk should be banished to Town A.

Town B has always been like this. The governing fathers (and some of the mothers) take great pride in their ability to dig football-size holes in the ground and place their heads gently in them, leaving their backsides visible and available for anyone to park their bikes.

They consider this a vital community service.

They hate change. It makes them nervous. It brings them out in hives.

But there are those in Town B who secretly love the idea.

Now…nearby, an even larger town is being built. It's not far short of completion.

This new town (we'll call it Town C for the sake of argument), won't produce any phlegm at all. Nobody will feel the need to spit anywhere.

It will have a choice of all the technology and benefits of the modern age…or very little technology at all. It will have modern homes, ideal office space, successful businesses, wonderful shopping malls, beautiful woods and streams, yoga classes, areas of natural boredom, top advertising agencies, talented creatives, materialistic consumers, and very thrifty consumers with sensible shoes and no credit cards.

It will have hot spots for technophiles and cold spots for luddites. It will have lots of plug sockets for laptop and mobile chargers…and lots of paper, pencils, pens and ink, for list makers and letter writers.

It will have sales folk who know what you want to buy before you know you want to buy it. And others who won't sell you anything unless they're absolutely sure you're totally interested in thinking about maybe looking at it.

Town C's businesses will have highly targeted marketing activities exclusively for the folk they want to talk to…and bugger all for the folk they don't. They won't have big budgets, but they will have big results.

Town C will have some folk who think that today is the best thing since sliced bread. And others who think that anything to do with tomorrow is automatically the dog's bollocks.

They'll all have the chances they need to move forward in life, as well as all the opportunities to stay exactly where they are.

There's a rumour going around that towns A and B will shortly have lots of properties up for sale…

Lonely old man or loveable Mog?

I missed an important anniversary.

It happened at 8.12pm on September 22nd, 2016. I can't even remember what I was doing. I might have been having my head looked at. The memory's a bit vague. Maybe that explains a lot.

It was the kind of anniversary that, if you're in the ad game, at least warranted a slight celebration. Maybe even a few fireworks. Definitely a raising of the odd glass or three.

The occasion? At that time…on that day…in 1955…the first ever advert was televised on UK TV, on the new ITV network. (2)

There are still some who wish it had been the last.

It won the spot by coming first in a competition. There were 23 other ads in the running, including ones for Guinness, Surf, National Benzole, Brown & Polson Custard, and Summer County Margarine.

Viewers saw a tube of toothpaste embedded in a block of ice, to the slogan: "It's tingling fresh. It's fresh as ice. It's Gibbs SR toothpaste."

Catchy, eh?

I was four years old and, by all accounts, a right little bugger. If my parents saw the ad at all, it would have been on a screen smaller than my iPad.

It would have been in black and white.

I would have been in bed and asleep.

Fast forward sixty years and I've just finished watching a gaggle of the latest feel-good Christmas ads on my very large flat screen telly.

After all this time, it seems the odour of stiff competition is still in the air.

Leading the pack was Man On The Moon, the new John Lewis offering, sponsored by Age UK, which has inspired thousands to volunteer to help the elderly during the festive season. Fetch the tissues!

I thought it was a dead cert winner. Until I saw the Sainsbury's "Mog" ad.

Accompanying this is a new book about Mog's Christmas adventures, and all profits are being donated to a Save The Children-led campaign to help kids become better readers. Brilliant!

Now all bets are off and Twitter is, apparently, going bonkers.

How many stuffed "Mog" soft toys Sainsbury's will sell is anyone's guess.

Look out Sergei and Oleg.

One thing's for sure, though.

John Lewis might not sell as many telescopes or lunar maps (if they even have any).

But they'll still get my vote.

For some, their ad might come in a close creative second.

But I suspect more than a few old folk couldn't give a damn.

As long as they're not alone this Christmas…

I needed a fix...fast.

There's no doubt about it. The world wide web is the best thing since sliced bread...and the worst thing since tight lycra shorts were squeezed onto very overweight people.

The internet has revolutionised the way things are done in just about every business, industry, and organisation worldwide.

It has invaded our homes, our families, the way we interact with each other, the way we buy, sell, browse, and communicate in every way, including word of mouth.

It's used by about 42% of the world's population. That's about 3.2 BILLION people. (3)

If the dog's bollocks and the bee's knees were ever to join together in the same body, it would be that!

Along with social networking, it has probably made us happier, faster, more satisfied, more successful, more productive, more cost effective, more inventive, more creative, more proactive, more motivated, more connected, more intertwined, more involved, more excited, more energised, more intimate, and more knowledgeable than we've ever been in our entire history.

But...

I suspect it has also made us more irritated, more lonely, more scared, more dejected, more furious, more jealous, more sad, more bitter, more left out, more left over, more left behind, more unfulfilled, more pissed off, more screwed up, more down in the dumps, and more dumped on our arses.

Sunday, I was wallowing in some of the former. A happy surfer. Soaking up information by osmosis through the spongy tips of my fingers.

But not yesterday…

That's when I experienced some of the latter. The downside. That's when I came off my drug of choice. When I went cold turkey. When I got the chills. The shakes. The jitters.

That's when my internet supply went down. Dried up. Rolled over and sodding died.

I did nothing wrong. I wasn't to blame. And yet, like a good Catholic, I assumed that somehow it was naturally all my fault.

I disconnected things. I waited. I reconnected things. Zilch. Nada. Not a bastard dicky bird. I needed a fix. Fast.

So I phoned up my service provider. I won't say who it is, but let's just say they've never had sex of any kind.

First they said I'd be back online by lunchtime. Then it was mid-afternoon. Then it was tea time. Then it was 7.00pm.

I knew they were doing their best to fix things. I knew they didn't like anything going wrong. And I knew that when anything went wrong they liked making it right it as quickly as possible. That's what they said. That's what they always say. They're very predictable.

But the curious thing was that, while they were in a state of fixing things, I was in a state of not needing them fixed. I was getting used to being an analogue creature again.

I was getting used to staring at a blank screen. It was almost hypnotic.

Before long, I was slipping back into writing copy on paper. With a pen. With no electronic grammar check. No spellcheck. It was quite soothing. Quite refreshing. Even quite exciting.

Until my new iPhone 6 Plus beeped. The one with 4G.

The one that said I had email.

The one that said I had internet capability.

My digital brain kicked in. Bugger analogue, I thought. Surf's up…

I love Macs.

I'm a creative. I love Macs. Hate PCs.

It's irrational, I know. Maybe even unkind.

But there's something about a PC that reminds me of my school dinners.

The ones served up before naked little Jamie Oliver was a twinkle in his dear old dad's eye.

School dinners to me were a necessary evil. I knew they were food, of a sort. I knew that somewhere deep inside they had vitamins and minerals. Give or take.

Occasionally they showed a smattering of good taste. Most of the time, however, they didn't give a damn whether I liked them or not.

They were made by people who had more regard for quantity rather than quality. And they were served up by people who had more regard for filling my plate than satisfying my appetite.

My taste buds were not big fans.

Then there's the Mac.

A PC is a personal computer in a dimly-lit room. A Mac is a whole new place in the sun.

There's something about a Mac that reminds me of Alison Thompson.

Alison…a beautiful, bold, forward-thinking 12-year-old who opened locked doors for me. In walls I never even knew were there.

I was 11. She was an older woman.

Alison…who showed me what excitement in a single touch felt like. Behind the bike shed. Before a shared No.6 cigarette.

Alison…who taught me how to be creative before I even knew the word existed.

Alison…who had style before she had O-levels.

Is a PC a damned fine computer? Absolutely. No doubt about it.

Does it have as much ability, charm, intelligence, focus, fun, imagination, and personality as a Mac?

Does it exist in the same creative universe, never mind the same damned ballpark, as a Mac?

Long silence….

Someone asked me not so long ago why so many writers and art directors seemed to prefer Macs to PCs.

I smiled and thought of Alison Thompson.

Bill Bernbach is alive...again!

I'd forgotten all about Bill Bernbach.
I know. When you're a copywriter, even a half-decent one, it's not the sort of name you forget easily. I apologise.
It's the sort of name that should, by rights, sear itself into the part of your brain reserved for things you should always do. Without even thinking.
Like breathing.
In the world of advertising giants, he was bigger, and a damned sight better, than most.
He's been gone since 1982, cruelly consigned to the back of my mind, gathering dust.
Until yesterday.
That's when he was brought back to life, here on Linkedin, by creator and strategist Kelvin Tillinghast. Nicely done, Kelvin!
That's when Kelvin posted Bill's resignation letter from Grey, in 1947. Sixty eight years ago. Two years before he co-founded Doyle Dane Bernbach.
It could easily have been written sixty eight minutes ago.
Here's just a taste:
"In the past year I must have interviewed about 80 people – writers and artists. Many of them from the so-called giants of the agency field. It was appalling to see how few of these people were genuinely creative. Sure, they had advertising know-how. Yes, they were up on advertising techniques. But look beneath the technique and what did you find? A sameness, a mental weariness, a mediocrity of ideas.

"It's that creative spark that I'm so jealous of for our agency and that I am so desperately fearful of losing. I don't want academicians. I don't want scientists. I don't want people who do the right things. I want people who do inspiring things."

Do yourself and your colleagues a big favour. Read the whole letter. You'll find it here. http://bit.ly/2pYawu9.

Then do yourself a bigger favour. Print it out and put it on a wall, where everyone can see it as they come in and go out.

Make it a condition of entry and exit that everyone reads it at least once.

Not just because the words and thoughts expressed have stood the test of time.

Not just because every single person who reads them can learn something worth learning.

But because if we don't read them…and if we don't learn from them…our creative arteries will harden.

We'll lose the spark that lit the flame.

We'll forget what inspired us to come into advertising in the first place.

But thankfully not all of us. Hopefully not even most of us.

Not if Bill Bernbach has anything to say about it.

He might have passed on. But for those of us who know, and those of us who have just been booted in the arse and reminded, he's still very much alive.

And kicking…

I'm old school...and new school.

I love words.
Every last one of them.
Short, long, thin, fat, words of every shape and size.
I love the way they roll off the tongue, pass between the lips, and introduce themselves to the air around us.
I'm old school. Because I love the magic that words have always been able to do...when people with grey hair, who love words as much as I do, put them on paper or on screen much better than I ever could.
I'm new school. Because I love how words can change our lives and change with the times...when people with fewer years tucked under their belt than I have, show me that tomorrow can be even more exciting than today.
I've always thought that the cleverest agencies around are the ones who can take old blood and new blood and let them both run freely through the same vein...in the same space...at the same time...with the same passion.
It really is a bit of a no-brainer.
The same goes for images.
I love art directors (remember them?) who bollock writers for writing too much copy.
I love them for their immovable infatuation with simplicity and beauty and space and impact.
I love them for bringing to life products and services for clients of every size and shape, that stick in the memory like superglue and can only be removed by ripping away too many layers of bloody skin.

I also love art directors who give writers free rein to tell a story in a way that can only be told by filling all the available space with beautiful type.

In fact, show me a Mac and I'll tell you I love anyone who can make technology perform magic...and turn plastic and metal into the road that leads to the things wishes and dreams are made of.

Because that's what advertising is all about.
Wishes and dreams.
More than big sales and new ideas.
Wishes and dreams.
More than big data and new media.
Wishes and dreams.
Always has been...hopefully always will be...

Black Friday punch-ups? Sod that...I'm British!

Something's rotten in the state of Denmark...
I love the idea of giving folk the chance to buy what they need for less than they thought.
I love the idea of letting them know about the latest gadget...the latest bargain...the latest sale...
I love the idea of helping them save millions of retail pounds, so they can spend them again just before Christmas...or just after it in the January Sales...and be well chuffed!
But I'm a bit iffy about watching them take part in hyperstore punch-ups to do it. A good saving, in my book, does not go hand in hand with a good kicking.
Not so long ago we were a queuing nation. A nation of polite shoppers. A nation of folk who patiently waited in line to get the biggest saving on the latest wide screen telly. A nation that knew what it was like to keep their fists firmly in their pockets and their tempers firmly in check.
I liked, even respected, our ability to rein in our desire to trample our fellow man, or woman, into the dust.
Then we changed.
We turned into a baying, frenzied mob. Wide-eyed and foaming at the mouth. Stamping over the broken bones of those in front of us.
Kicking, punching and gouging our way to the shelves before there was nowhere left to go and nothing left to buy.
Or at least some of us did.

The rest of us, I'm delighted to say, took one look at the physical carnage of Black Friday and thought: bugger this for a game of soldiers…we're British, goddammit.

We want a more refined retail punch up.

We want safer, more cerebral blood and guts.

We want to keep in the black without being in the blue.

We want a digital rush…not a kick, bollock scramble.

We want to stay in and log on…not queue up and get pissed off.

Cue the Mamas and the Papas.

Cyber Monday…so good to me…

Talent never dies.

I knew a drummer who hated drum kits.

He was a Cuban (from the arse-end of Glasgow) and his instruments of choice were a selection of beautiful wooden congas.

They had natural skin heads.

He could never get used to the idea of bashing the Hell out of a kit with sticks.

To him, rhythm was a living thing. A life force. And the only way to get close enough to that rhythm to truly feel it was to use the palms of his hands.

Skin on skin.

He was a bit of a purist.

He was also a bit of an alcoholic, but that's a different story.

The point is, he wasn't just a musician. He was a magician.

He could make those skins talk or sing. Moan, laugh, or cry. And in the process, bring back to life something that used to belong to a cow.

For him, no advances in percussive technology could take the place of the human body. His body.

He didn't get much work. Time, it seemed, was passing him by.

Coincidentally, I knew a visualiser (remember them?), who thought the same way.

He came from the North of England and he thought that anyone who tried to visualise anything on a computer was missing the bloody point.

He loved Guinness. But like the Cuban, that's a different story.

To him, the only way to visualise was to get close to the paper with his fingers and a damned fine set of pencils, pens, and magic markers.

To him, talent was God-given…not Mac given. To him, it lived in the brain…not in some damned silicon chip.

Over the years the number of agencies using him got less and less. And the number of talented Mac designers in those agencies got more and more.

Pretty soon, Mac visuals were all that the agency clients wanted to see. They didn't want hand-drawn ones.

The visualiser thought about leaving the ad business completely and retiring to a life of fine art and a smaller bank balance. Or a job at B&Q.

Then a curious thing happened.

The Agencies missed the scribbles…the first thoughts…the initial ideas…the slick visuals.

As did their clients.

So his phone started ringing again.

He even found himself working alongside those Mac designers he used to dislike so much. Then another curious thing happened.

He found that he had a grudging (and growing) respect for them and the work they did.

The feeling was mutual.

They liked the visuals he made.

And he realised that what sat between his ears was a damned sight more important than what sat between his fingers.

Curiously enough, the same thing was happening a few hundred miles to the North, where an ageing Cuban conga player started getting regular gigs with a band full of young, talented, musicians.

They liked the sound he made.

Talent never dies.

It just learns to adapt…

The genie is out of the bottle.

An extremely good friend of mine recently became a Facebook convert.

He seems to have turned a corner in his growing appreciation of social media.

He did dabble in Linkedin. Purely on a business basis. Until now, the casual, ad-libbing, friendly warmth of Facebook was purely Satan's territory.

Not any more.

He didn't exactly have a Saul on the road to Damascus moment.

His was more a Manfred Mann moment.

He was blinded by the light.

When his eyes cleared he had well and truly joined the hordes of digital believers in an internet populated by 3.2 BILLION users worldwide. [4]

Give or take.

I was reminded of his conversion when, the other day, someone (I can't remember who…but whoever you are, "Thank you") kindly posted an infographic of the number of social media users operating online every minute of the day.

It contained the kind of statistics (yeah…I know….lies…damned lies…and statistics) that, depending on which side of the fence you stood, either delighted you, or scared the shit out of you.

I'm sitting on the fence…and it's a real pain in the arse.

However, so far, I'm still keeping my shit well and truly in.

Yay me.

Don't get me wrong. Although half of me thinks I was born a few centuries too late, the other half is pissed off because it thinks I was born a few centuries too early.

The trick is figuring out which half is which.

The latest numbers say that Facebook users post over 4 MILLION 'likes' every minute of the day.

And during the same time, Pinterest users 'pin' nearly 10,000 images…Twitter users send nearly 350,000 'tweets'…and YouTube users upload around 300 hours of new video! [4]

I'll say it again. EVERY MINUTE OF THE DAY!

And that's just the tip of the iceberg.

There's also Uber, Skype, Buzzfeed, Snapchat, Tinder, Vine, Amazon, Reddit, Netflix, Apple, and Instagram.

And they're all on steroids!!

In fact while you're reading this, BILLIONS of people will be pinning, posting, skyping, swiping, snapping, loading…and helping the world communicate easier, faster, and more effectively than it has ever done before.

And they won't just be doing it for pleasure.

Businesses (at least those working at moving forward) use these platforms to help change the way they make decisions not only about their own futures, but also about the way their clients do business.

But the world is not only becoming smaller…it's becoming noisier, smarter, faster, friendlier, more intrusive, more inventive, more transparent, more thoughtless, more thoughtful, more connected, more disconnected, more lazy, more egocentric, more sociable, more safe, more dangerous, more businesslike, more free, more controlling, more productive, less productive…the list goes on and on!

And it's becoming harder and harder to turn our electronic devices off.

Harder and harder to remember what it was like before we switched them on in the first place.

I soddin' hate it.

I bloody love it.

We have let the genie out of the bottle.
We have become a digital species.
Peel back our skin and see our motherboards…

Creativity is rearing its beautiful head.

Not so long ago, I thought it was in hiding.
Drawbridge up. Hatches battened.
Fed up of all the loud, bullying, poor excuses for creativity that poured out of agencies of all shapes and sizes.
Too embarrassed to be mentioned in the same breath as the dross that was shoved in the faces of readers and viewers who were conditioned, even brainwashed, to believe that what they read and saw was the best there was.
The best that the great minds in the marketing world could come up with.
But I was wrong.
It was scheming.
Plotting.
Girding its loins.
Sharpening its teeth.
Getting itself ready to kick some crap creative arse.
Now it has its kicking boots on.
I can feel the rumblings. Like a once-dormant volcano announcing its presence to all who had forgotten it existed.
I can see the geyser-like escapings of wonderful thinking. Bursting through the surface and surprising the hell out of anyone within reading, listening, and gasping distance.
The beautiful creatures in the creative departments have figured out how to remove their straitjackets. It was only a matter of time.
They're remembering what it feels like to believe in themselves again.
They're remembering what it feels like to stand up and fight tooth and nail for their ideals. And their ideas.

Ideas that once fell by the wayside because they were considered too risky by those who weren't intelligent enough to recognise a great thought if it bit them on the arse.

They're remembering the kind of originality that used to light a fire in the belly. Bring a tear to the eye. A smile to the heart. A tingle to the spine.

They're remembering the kind of snarling, protective bravery that shoved two fingers up to those who dared to take real advertising and stuff it in a locked room with no windows. And no fresh air.

They're remembering the kind of creative departments that were larger than life. The kind that gave birth to people who became legends. With campaigns that moved mountains and were remembered for decades.

They're remembering how to flex their muscles again.

And God help anyone who thinks that good enough really is good enough…

Ho...Ho...Ho.

I've never had a great memory.
It's selective. It remembers what it thinks is important. What it thinks is interesting. What it thinks is potentially useful.
And promptly forgets the rest.
It remembers faces.
It's useless with names.
It remembers some facts with a passion. And lets others slip through the cracks to disappear into the void.
I think maybe that's why I love advertising that tells a good story. Advertising that triggers an emotional response somewhere between my ears and behind my ribs.
I love getting lost in the tale.
The problem is that sometimes the tale outweighs the reason for telling it in the first place.
So I tend to remember the marvellous Mog...and push Sainsbury's into the background.
The same goes with excellent, tear-jerking Man On The Moon...and John Lewis.
I do remember the brilliant Aldi version...although for other reasons.
Neuro-Insight's winner for Christmas this year was the Burberry ad, celebrating 15 years of Billy Elliot. (Read the article published in Campaign on December 7th).
Very sparkly. Full of fun and celebrity. But if they were going to do it properly, where the Hell was Jamie Bell?
Sorry Burberry (and Neuro-Insight). It was stylish...but about as warm and festive as a wet fart in a Santa suit.

My pick...and it will probably be way down low on most other lists...was an image I saw a week or so ago. On Facebook.

Picture this.

Neutral background. Three Hovis loaves. Nothing more.

Each one almost covering the one behind.

All you could see of the brand name rising out of the uncut bread, was the beginning of the word Hovis.

Two letters. Times three.

Ho. Ho. Ho.

Bloody simple. Bloody brilliant. And branding at its bloody best.

All for the price of a decent photographer...three uncut loaves...and the kind of lightbulb moment that any self-respecting creative would murder their granny for.

Merry Christmas...

Tell them a story.

There are those in this business who think that the only true point of advertising is to get clients' customers to part with their hard-earned dosh.

Hopefully as much of it as possible. As often as possible.

Anything else surely belongs in the realms of artistic claptrap.

Anything else is surely just creativity disappearing up its own backside.

Anything else surely involves meaningless award ceremonies where smiling folk with more money than talent pat each other on the back. Silently wishing they could slide a sneaky dagger between their opponents' ribs without spilling a drop of precious blood on their own tux or gown.

Goddammit…this is a RESULTS BUSINESS!! A sales business. A profit business. A hard-nosed numbers game. A bottom line for bean counters.

You think it's anything different? Go think it somewhere else. And don't let the door hit your arse on the way out.

Yeah…right.

Read my lips.

Bollocks!

The only true point of advertising is to make folk feel good.

Hopefully as good as possible. As often as possible.

They might feel good because they're spending money…because they're saving it…or because they're making it.

They might feel good because they've got what they want…or because they've got what they need.

They might feel good because something you said made them smile on the inside…or because something you did made them smile on the outside.

They might feel good because you make them laugh…or cry…or think…or remember…or get goosebumps…or disappear for a minute or two into their imagination.

They might feel good because the images you show them, or the words you write, touch them somewhere deep inside. Or answer a need. Or just make them go to bed at night feeling better than they did when they got up that morning.

It really doesn't matter.

If you can't make folk feel good about what you want to tell them…how the hell are they going to feel good about what you want to sell them.

So tell them a story.

Make it a good one.

And make sure it has a happy ending…

Respect.

A while ago, Marketing and Advertising Consultant and Copywriter Jim O'Connor posed the question, here on Linkedin, "Is copywriting undervalued?"

It followed a recent survey by the Direct Marketing Association which suggested that more than half of UK copywriters feel that there is a lack of respect for the value they bring to projects.

Nice piece, Jim. Very nice piece.

It got me thinking...

One; I think the most important kind of respect a writer (or art director...or anyone come to that) can rely on is good old self-respect. Not just for the person they are but also for the talent they have.

Two; far too many folk concentrate on the quantity of copy rather than the quality.

Three; everyone can write. Not everyone can write well. Even fewer can write very well. One or two deserve their own star on the sidewalk outside Sid Grauman's Chinese Theatre.

Four; good copywriters will always be highly regarded by those who really matter. Well...nearly always.

Five; copy doesn't just sell. It entertains, informs, touches hearts, changes minds. Sometimes even changes lives. And the distance between merely good and bloody great is just a different combination of 26 letters.

It's that simple. And that hard.

Six; the truth is ALWAYS more important than a cleverly-crafted lie. But not always as entertaining.

Seven; never, never, never, never, never, never, never, NEVER bore your audience.

Eight; if it's a choice between touching the wallet or the heart of customers, choose the heart. The wallet will follow.

Nine; never forget that good enough never is.

And then there's Ten.

If you don't value the words when you write them, why should anyone else value the products when they read about them?

Punctuated by a ding.

I feel like crying.
Or at least sighing...heavily.
I feel like it's the end of an era, which I suppose it is.
Like the last majestic beast of its kind in the world has finally popped its clogs, which it has.
I learned yesterday, via best-selling Crime Writer Ed Lynskey (thanks Ed), right here on Linkedin, that the last manual typewriter factory left in the world (it's in Mumbai) is closing its doors.
Forever.
The last one in the whole bloody world!
News like this should at least have a dramatic piece of music to accompany it.
Something from a Hitchcock movie, perhaps.
Something shocking.
Possibly accompanied by a sharp intake of breath and a wide-eyed stare.
Punctuated by a ding.
It feels like the kind of event that, one day, will be spoken about by old writers sitting round open fires and drinking rotgut whisky.
Remembering the way things used to be done.
With muscle power, ribboned ink, reams of paper, the odour of cleaning oil, and the noise of small, thin, mechanical arms moving in a comforting rhythm.
Remembering a time when typewriters were typewriters.
When they were works of art. Helping to create other works of art.

From the Remington Noiseless beast of Faulkner…to the famed, battered lightweight, Olivetti Lettera 32 of Cormac McCarthy.

And me.

I have three of them now. I used to have two. Not one of the buggers can write as well as McCarthy's.

Not even in the same universe.

It takes physical and mental effort to write anything worth shit with a manual typewriter.

Ever since I ran out of ribbons, I write solely on my Mac. I love it, of course. But it only takes mental effort. Lots of it.

Sometimes I like hearing the cogs go round on the outside, as well as on the inside.

My Mac is quietly digital…and I still hanker after a noisy analogue session every now and then.

Just to make the neighbours talk.

Just to balance things out.

Electricity and silicon chips have made the 'doing' bit too damned easy on the hands and heads.

And as my old tooth-pulling grandad used to say…if it comes out easy, you're doing it wrong.

There should be blood and pain involved. There should be aching pinkie fingers and throbbing migraines.

There should be split fingernails and frayed tempers.

There should be well-thumbed dictionaries. Not instant spellcheckers. Many crossings out. Not autocorrect. Bins full of screwed up paper balls. Not screens wiped clean as if by magic.

Perspiration as well as inspiration. Heights of joy as well as depths of despair.

There should be evidence of bloody effort.

At least for the first draft.

Maybe before they lock up shop and throw away the keys, they'll have a closing down sale. I wonder how much a flight would be from Manchester to Mumbai.

By turboprop airliner, of course…

Three little words.

There's a guy inside my head who speaks aloud all the ad copy I read.
Every line…every word…every syllable.
He does it with all the copy I write, too.
Doesn't matter how long or short it is.
How good or bad it is.
Doesn't matter whether it's full of facts, full of emotion, or just plain full of shit.
He starts at the first word, ends at the last word, and treats everything in between as if he's talking to a friend.
Me.
He doesn't have any airs or graces.
He doesn't like copy that reads like copy.
He doesn't like copy that sounds like selling.
He thinks some of the words aren't friendly. Not memorable. Not warm. Not true. Not genuine. Not enjoyable. Too pushy. Too clunky. Too arrogant. Too full of their own importance.
Too empty of anything that feels real.
It pisses him off.
But his job is to keep me on track. So he ignores the temptation to zip the lip.
Happily, he thinks a lot of the words are spot on. Bloody perfect. As real as a blush. Something you just can't fake.
When he reads those words I can hear his voice smile.
If he does it while he's reading any of my copy, I know I've done something at least half right.
I wish that happened more often.

If he does it when he's reading copy somebody else wrote, I know he's trying to tell me something.

Something really important.

Something wrapped up in those three little words I know so well.

Could try harder.

Bastard…

Want to be a creative? Get a fuzzy brain!

According to an article in The Scientific American, our brains do more creative work when we're tired. (5)

We think better out of the box, apparently, when our batteries are well and truly buggered.

When our brains are feeling decidedly fuzzy.

It's got something to do with filters and distractions and focus and stuff.

Here's how it works.

When we're tired, our brains aren't as good at filtering out distractions.

Result? Now about this headline....oooh, I could murder a pint!

In this case, distractions equals alcohol. Alcohol equals lowering of inhibitions and opening of doors we didn't even know were there in the first place.

When we're tired, our brains are less efficient at remembering connections between ideas and concepts.

Result? Emm...emm...emm...

Now...when THAT happens, our grey cells are bullied into making new connections.

Because we can't for the life of us remember the old ones.

There could even be exciting conceptual punch-ups involved.

New ideas and new ways of thinking shove their way into all our orifices.

Okay, maybe just some of them. Forcing us to pull our creative fingers out.

Result? Glorious lightbulb moments. Ridiculously fascinating off the wall ideas.

Maybe even a few freakish and fascinating combinations of unconventional words and images.

So…

Want to play safe?

Grab the Horlicks and get a good night's sleep.

Want to get creative?

Staple your eyelids open and develop a fuzzy brain.

Apparently…

There are four kinds of Christmas.

In the first kind of Christmas, unsurprisingly, really sensible folk get exactly what they want.

Let's call them "happy" for the sake of argument.

Life is good and Santa got the message.

This is the Christmas that ad agencies, clients and customers dream of.

The Christmas of dreams and profits. Where everything goes to plan and it snows right on cue on Christmas Eve.

The ghost of Jimmy Stewart even puts in an appearance.

Then there's the second kind of Christmas. Where really excited, but often disappointed, folk get precisely what other folk think they'd like.

Let's call them "re-gifters".

They're the ones who gush with joy right up until the moment they unwrap something they'd never buy for themselves in a million years.

There's no Santa involved here.

He must have taken a wrong turning at Albuquerque.

Then there's the third kind of Christmas. The kind reserved for the BILLIONS of folk who don't celebrate Christmas at all.

But somehow don't feel the worse for it.

They probably think the idea of flying reindeer and a laughing fat man in a red suit are just marketing gimmicks designed to part them from their hard-earned dosh. If they had any.

They might not be entirely wrong. But it makes a whole lot of folk from the first kind of Christmas very happy.

So yah boo sucks!

Then there's the last kind of Christmas.

The fourth kind.

This is the Christmas that takes care of the bodies, hearts and minds of those who are broken and need putting back together again.

If possible.

This is the Christmas reserved for all those too ill…too poor…too hungry…too oppressed…too forgotten…too lonely…too depressed…too homeless…too unfortunate…too threatened…too angry…too devastated…too lost…too torn apart…and too much in pain to enjoy any damned Christmas at all.

These are the folk so far down the hole they can't even see the light at the top anymore.

The fourth kind of Christmas is for them.

And it's the one I reserve my biggest, strongest, warmest, most heartfelt Christmas wishes for.

Because they're the folk who always need it the most…

Santa and me.

Santa was only twenty years old when I was born.

He came into the world fully grown, with his smiley face, ruddy cheeks, large waistline, snow-white beard, and fat red suit.

He was hairy, happy, full of the joys of life…and the best damned gift to festive advertising and marketing there had ever been.

He still is.

At the time, I was small, bald, full of shit, wind and noise…and one of the most enthusiastic end-users that cotton nappy manufacturers could ever wish for.

He, or at least the modern version of him, was created by Finish/American illustrator Haddon Sundblom [6] in December 1931, for the D'Arcy Ad Agency in St. Louis, USA.

The client was Coca Cola.

I, or at least the starter version of me, was created for a growing family by a lovely Scottish couple who always went by the names of Mum and Dad.

This new happy Santa has changed very little in the intervening years between then and now.

He's still overweight. Still says 'Ho Ho Ho'. Still wears red and white. Still thrills everyone around Christmas time. Still has a fondness for reindeer (we don't talk about that).

Still gives folk the world over another good reason to be nice to one another.

As for me…

I grew quickly out of nappies, slowly into adulthood, and joyfully, sometimes painfully, into a fairly reasonable facsimile of an advertising creative.

I've changed beyond all recognition from that small, inquisitive child who thought that Santa had a part-time job as my dad and smelled a lot like his best friend Uncle Johnny Walker.

Well…maybe not beyond ALL recognition.

The baldness seems to have returned.

Hopefully Santa will, too.

Which reminds me…

May all your festive wishes have the good sense to come true sooner rather than later.

May everyone you know greet you with a warm heart and an open mind. May life, with all its wonderful ingenuity give you every opportunity to feel better and do better in the coming new year.

And may the ones you love always find more reasons to love you with every breath in their body.

Have an extremely Merry Christmas, followed by a highly prosperous and Happy New Year.

And remember to leave something out for Santa before you go to bed on Christmas Eve.

Preferably something distilled north of the border…

I feel a great disturbance in The Force.

There must be something wrong with me.
I must be either physically lacking in some essential element, or I'm psychologically below par.
I can't seem to get excited about the new Star Wars movie.
I might be the victim of a sudden and serious character flaw.
Don't get me wrong.
It's not that I have no interest in movies.
Far from it. I think they're brilliant.
I've seen every Star Wars movie ever made, dozens of times.
Well…nearly every one.
If there was a Harrison Ford fan club nearby, I would probably be a loyal member.
I really love him.
Please don't read anything into that.
I wonder if it's a vitamin or mineral deficiency.
I do have an extremely low Vitamin B12 level.
I wonder if one of the symptoms is a sudden and irrational inability to appreciate the importance of everything George Lucas does.
Shit!! George Lucas is a giant.
I think he's brilliant.
If there was a George Lucas fan club nearby, I would probably be a loyal member.
I really love him.
Please don't read anything into that.
Maybe it's because it's Christmas.

Maybe the sheer scale of the festive celebrations is somehow overshadowing a movie of such epic proportions.

Maybe anything that happens in galaxies far far away naturally plays second fiddle to anyone dressed up in a fat Santa suit.

It's understandable.

I think Santa's brilliant.

I really love him.

Please don't read anything into that…

The birth of advertising...in 300 words.

Let's go back in time.

Back to a crossroads moment in history, when the first hunters decided to get together with the first gatherers and swap some of their hard-earned meat for some delicious looking root vegetables.

This swap thing was a new concept to both tribes.

But the bright spark who thought of it was the favourite daughter of the meat-eating chief, so naturally all her tribe thought it was a great idea.

The hunters, keen to get the best deal for their freshly butchered victims, no doubt boasted about its quality.

The veggie growers probably did the same, although they were more modest folk. They'd always fancied some meat with their greens.

The cannier of them argued that refusal to deal might result in a midnight raid with painful consequences. And some of these consequences might involve not feeling any pain at all. Ever again.

Self-preservation was an old concept to both tribes.

After much haggling, the very first retail deal was struck, and both parties went their separate ways.

Pretty soon, the meat eaters sent out folk to tell the veggie eaters when a new supply of choice flesh was ready to be bartered for.

The veggie growers, wishing to appear just as helpful, did the same.

Sometimes these messengers would return in triumph, with news of many potential customers eager to have variety in their diets.

Sometimes they would never be heard of again.

A few hundred thousand years later, this messenger practice is still going on.

Only now it's not called risking your life and learning how to run very fast.

It's called Advertising.

Get it wrong, and the only thing you'll lose is your reputation.

And possibly some customers.

And occasionally your shirt.

Get it right, and the only thing you'll gain is everything…

The return of The Spider.

Some things never die.
They just fade into the background and sit there. Waiting.
From the moment I picked up a coloured crayon and dragged it across some paper all those years ago (hang on…better make that decades ago), I was hooked. Captivated. Addicted.
At the time, I didn't know what the squiggly marks meant, if indeed they meant anything.
But I knew that creating them made me feel good.
Later, and with the help of a half-decent imagination, some of those squiggles became pretty decent drawings.
The rest of them, however, went on a very different journey.
I was ten (give or take) when I was introduced to Robert Louis Stevenson.
That was when it all kicked off.
There are doors in your life that you knock on politely, turn the handle, and open slowly. Like an examination room in a doctor's surgery.
There are doors you run up to and barge open with your shoulder. Without a second's thought for the consequences. Or the pain.
And then there are the other doors. The clever ones. The ones that look right at you. Size you up. Come to a decision. Then open right up without being asked.
Almost as if they know something you don't.
I was given a battered copy of Treasure Island.

One of the clever doors opened (I didn't even know the wall was there, never mind the damned door), and someone called Jim Hawkins invited me in.

I didn't think twice.

I always loved reading.

Pretty soon after that I realised I also loved writing.

That's when I met The Spider.

He wasn't neat. He wasn't tidy. He wasn't anything like the careful, bendy, cursive creature I met in primary school.

He was a wild, scampering animal who raced across the page, scratching words and sentences as he went. Leaving chaos and confusion in his wake.

Cursive was his careful, boring cousin. Cursive was too slow to keep up with my thinking. Cursive was first gear. I wanted to travel in fifth.

The Spider became my best friend. My literary buddy. My creative companion on the road to wherever my imagination decided to take me.

Nobody understood him like I did. Nobody understood me like he did. Everything was hunky dory. Except for one thing.

I began to need more speed. More digit dexterity. He began to need more rests. More thoughtful time-outs. He was easily knackered. I needed a sixth gear.

So I learned how to type. And somewhere in all the rampant technology of analogue and digital keyboards, the spider got lost. Left behind. Forgotten.

I was like the wind. The words flew from my machine like an alphabetical Usain Bolt. Everything was tickety-boo. Except for one thing.

Pretty soon my words began to overtake my thoughts. My sentences were fifty per cent cream and fifty per cent crap. More often than not my paragraphs flew into the bin, not onto the page.

Something was missing.

Then, this Christmas, a kind and wise soul bought me a beautiful Waterman fountain pen.

The ink was black as coal. The nib was smooth as silk.

I wrote some copy today. The first draft. Just a couple of pages.

As I was writing I could feel the soft stirrings of my old friend The Spider. Only now he wasn't moving at his usual breakneck speed.

He was taking his time.

Allowing me to take mine.

The ink he left on the page was tall dark and handsome.

And the last eleven words were these:

Faster just gives you more words.

Slower gives you better thinking.

Nice…

Pin back your ears...it's Trotty Time

There's a lot of crap talked about the ad game.

Sometimes by folk on the outside. Sometimes by folk on the inside.

Most of them wouldn't know their creative arse from their elbow.

Unlike Dave Trott.

He's the kind of guy you listen to if you want to find out how things should be done.

He's the kind of guy you should have listened to before you listened to anyone else in the first place.

He's the kind of creative who make folk want to come into advertising and try to be as creative as him.

We're still trying.

So switch on your web browser. Look for an IPA Podcast called Dave Trott in Conversation. Grab yourself a coffee. Sit back. And for 28 minutes, listen to someone who's been there, done that, got the t-shirt, worn it, torn it, and probably used it to polish his car.

Or read his articles published in Campaign online.

He's a bit of a legend.

Well...actually he's a lot of a legend.

He's also a one-man masterclass in creative thinking.

After starting his career at BMP he founded a number of agencies including Gold Greenlees Trott, Bainsfair Sharkey Trott and Chick Smith Trott.

Some folk deserve to be remembered.

Others you have no damned right to forget...

It's the beginning of the end.

In a few days it will be the end of the beginning.

There's an out with the old, in with the new, kind of feeling about the place.

At some point a raising (and emptying) of the alcohol-filled glasses will be performed. Repeatedly.

Followed by a reflection on the year we left behind.

We'll quietly, or loudly, hope that the year we're about to enter will be more of the same, or a damned sight better because it couldn't get any worse.

Some of us will go through the motions of making our resolutions. Knowing well that we don't have a skinny cat in Hell's chance of keeping all of them.

But we'll try.

Just to start the ball rolling, here are some of mine.

I'll be kinder to those who don't think that the creative department is the heart of the agency.

It's not their fault. They know not what they say.

I'll try to remember that good enough is never good enough.

I'll never forget that there's a difference between creativity and marketing. And long may that remain.

I'll look with pity on anyone who doesn't believe that the idea is king.

I'll try to convince them that everything else is just a collection of different ways of making the idea come to life.

I won't always succeed.

I'll throw the decaf coffee in the bin. I tried it for a year and it's time to go back to the real stuff.

I'll always remember that analogue still has a big role to play in a digital world.

I'll pray that writers and art directors continue to be given the time and space to create words and pictures that make clients' customers stop and look…not stop looking.

Yes…I did say writers and art directors.

I'll consider euthanasia if I ever get too boring.

I'll accept the fact that some things change.

I'll also accept the fact that some things will stay reassuringly the same.

I'll learn more about clients.

I'll learn more about myself.

I realise that the former may lead to the latter.

I also realise that the latter may lead to the former.

I'll hope that those coming into advertising are taught how to do things properly, instead of being thrown in at the deep end and only given jobs if they can swim like Michael Phelps.

Google him.

I'll smile more…argue less…and add something extra to every brief I get.

I'll never forget that real creativity is worth a damned sight more than the sum of its individual parts.

I'll remember that, sometimes, speaking is just noise…and, sometimes, silence is full of all the right words.

That's all for now folks.

See you on the flip side…

Here we go again.

We've turned the corner and welcomed in another New Year.

So...will the world be a better place today than it was yesterday?

Will the fact that it's 2016 instead of 2015 make a blind bit of difference to the lives of any of us?

Will I be happier?

Will I win the Lottery jackpot?

Will I wake up tomorrow with a larger bank balance or smaller ears?

God only knows, and he ain't telling. But I do know this.

There are 7.5 BILLION [7] of us stuck on this little rock hurtling through space at 67,000 miles an hour [8] (give or take). Somewhere near the arse end of a small, insignificant galaxy.

If we play our cards right and don't piss off anyone who just happens to have a bigger stick, we might actually make it.

It might be a close fight...but my money's on the gimp with the bent nose and the heart of gold.

He does his best work on a Monday.

But this isn't just any old Monday.

It's not even an M&S Monday.

It's the Monday when you develop a small ache in your heart and a large ache in your dominant hand.

The small ache is caused by a slight tug in the left ventricle (or it might be the right one), when you realise you've left something behind when you came to work this morning.

It's called last year.

Don't worry. You'll soon get over it. The medicine you need is everywhere around you.

It's called this year.

The large ache is caused by a hefty compression of the muscles in the fingers and palm of your dominant hand.

It happens when you smile and shake the hands of everyone you can see when you walk through the office door first thing this morning.

And wish them Happy New Year.

You do it with gusto. There may even be pain involved.

Don't worry. You'll soon get over that, too. The medicine you need is everywhere around you.

It's called switching your brain on again and getting back to work.

It might take you a minute or two. It might take you all week.

Some brains take longer to switch back on than others.

That's what coffee's for.

Welcome to 2016…

Kensitas coupons, creativity, and Jeff Goldblum.

When my mother was alive she used to smoke.

Perhaps that's why, when she died, she chose to be buried, rather than cremated.

Maybe she fancied a change.

Anyway, her smoking brand of choice was Kensitas.

It was a long time ago.

I asked her once why she smoked them. (My father smoked Senior Service). I expected her to say that they tasted better than all the others. Or because they were cheaper. Or because she liked the colourful packets.

She said it was because every pack contained coupons. She could exchange them for free gifts. She had a stack of coupons.

That was my introduction to effective marketing.

I was about 10 or 11 at the time.

When I was about 12 or 13, the doctor gave her a choice. She could carry on smoking and, pretty soon, be carried out of the house in a box…or stop smoking and carry on living.

Or words to that effect.

She chose the latter and stopped overnight.

That was my introduction to effective healthcare.

A doctor scaring the shit out of you does more good than an advertising copywriter trying to make you feel good. At least where my mother was concerned.

The trouble is…most folk just want to feel exactly that. Good. They want to run with the pack. They want to be in the company of like-minded individuals.

They don't want to be Johnny No Mates.
You're never alone with a Strand.
That was my introduction to the human condition.
We want to be let in the door…not left out in the cold.
At least most of us.
There were a few of us who preferred being different. On the outside looking in.
Trouble is, being different grew to be cool. And the few grew into the many.
And pretty soon there were more on the outside than on the inside.
And then we realised that it didn't matter one iota where we were. Or how cool we looked.
We couldn't run. We couldn't hide.
We were consumers…and the folks in the marketing department had us by the short and curlies.
All we could do was sit back, pay up, and try to enjoy the ride.
Luckily, that's when Advertising walked in the door.
Strutted probably.
Artistic and literate. Clever and flashy. Entertaining and funny. Persuasive and thought-provoking. Brave and brash.
Pretty soon we didn't want to run. We didn't want to hide. And we sure as hell didn't want it to stop.
We enjoyed it. Revelled in it, even.
Guinness was good for us. Or at least some of us.
Just do it, we thought.
But nothing good lasts for ever, right?
After a while, bean counters with grey suits, boring spectacles and about as much creativity as a trod-on chip came in and took over the decision-making.
That was my introduction to going cold turkey.
Happily, this didn't last long either. Well…not very.
The wheel always turns.

There's a scene in the first Jurassic Park movie where Jeff Goldblum is told that the dinosaurs in the park can't replicate because they're all created female.

His response is a wise: "Life will not be contained. Life breaks free."

Creativity's the same.

Try to hold it down and it will rise up and bite you in the arse.

Creativity will not be contained. Creativity breaks free.

Only this time its teeth are sharper.

Its roar is louder.

And it has one hell of an appetite…

Complicated is the new simple.

Picture this...
It's the dim (and distant) past.
You're a humble stallholder in a local market.
Your customers are the folk who stop at your stall long enough to buy what you have to sell.
You have what they want, so they know where to come.
You know a little bit about some of them (your regulars). Most of them you know bugger all about.
They turn up, fork out, move on.
Your idea of being proactive is smiling at them hopefully.
Now, fast forward into the present day and picture another scene.
You're the successful descendant of a poor stallholder. You own a large supermarket chain. It stretches from one end of the country to the other.
Each of your stores stocks thousands of items and together you have millions of customers.
You have what they want, so they know where to come.
Your idea of being proactive is making sure that you offer them the best goods at the best prices. You can't go wrong.
You have a highly talented marketing department...run by a highly talented Marketing Director...and he has hired a highly talented advertising agency.

You're presented with the agency's latest ad campaign ideas and you're highly pissed off.

It's a little yesterday. Well...a lot older than that, actually.

"Hang on a skinny minute," you say, one eyebrow slightly more annoyed than the other. "All you're doing is telling customers what we did in the past," you say. "It's very nice and retro...but aren't we sort of preaching to the converted?"

"Customers these days aren't very loyal," says the highly talented Agency's Creative Director. "They need to be engaged. You need to tell them your story," he says.

"But we've got the best goods at the best prices," you say. "Isn't that a good enough story?"

"They need to warm to you and enjoy coming into your stores," he says.

"But we've got the best goods at the best prices. We're not warm...we're bloody red hot," you say.

"Aaah...but you need to give them time to browse and consider and compare," he says.

"But we've got the best goods at the best prices. Consider THAT," you say. You begin to get even more pissed off.

You look at the agency bill. The new campaign will cost MILLIONS of pounds. It's funny...sort of.

"A little light humour always goes down well," he says. "Help them smile and you'll help them buy."

"Bollocks!" you say. "Help them SAVE and you'll help them buy. Forget about the past...what about the future?"

"The future is so yesterday," he says. "The past is where tomorrow's at!"

"What about today?" you say.

"Digital changes everything," he said.

You look at the hands on your Timex analogue chronograph.

"Tell me more," you say.

"Behavioural profiling," he says.

"What the bloody hell does the FBI have to do with my customers?" you say.

He frowns. "Think online…think Google…think Yahoo," he says.

"What about offline?" you say.

"Online is the new offline," he says

"It all sounds very dear," you say.

"Dear is the new cheap," he says.

Suddenly a simpler life seems attractive. You wish you were a humble stallholder in a local market.

"So…behavioural profiling, eh? What else?" you say.

"We have algorithms," he says.

"They sounds complicated," you say.

"Complicated is the new simple," he says.

"What's more simple than telling folk we have the best goods at the best prices?" you say.

I'm not a Bingeaholic.

I had a nightmare last night.

I was in a room full of people.

All bleary-eyed through lack of sleep. All suffering from a palpable lack of anticipation. All wishing they were somewhere else.

There was a man standing in front of the crowd. Sweating heavily. In the throes of cold turkey. He began to speak.

"Hello, my name is Arthur, and I'm a Bingeaholic," he said.

"Hello Arthur," said the crowd as one.

Then Arthur began to tell his story.

He used to be like other folk, normal folk, he said. He used to watch telly most nights, after tea, when he got home from work.

He used to look forward to every episode of his favourite programmes. Mostly they had something to do with wholesale bloody murder.

He was a pacifist.

He used to talk about them with his workmates.

They used to have long conversations about who killed who, why and who was going to get killed off next week.

Then somebody told him about live streaming with Netflix and Hulu and Amazon Prime.

"Why don't you try streaming your episodes and you can watch them all one after the other", they said. "Bugger all that waiting around," they said.

"Best of all," they said, "you don't have to watch any bloody adverts if you don't want to!"

Arthur felt his pulse quicken just a tad. No more waiting. No more wondering.

So he tried it. And he loved it.

He couldn't get enough of it.

In no time at all he was a hardened binge viewer.

He spent every waking moment working, watching or sleeping. Pretty soon he was falling asleep at his job, which he lost.

Then he began throwing illegal substances down his neck at an alarming rate, just to keep himself awake. Just to keep watching.

He was a wreck, but like all good Bingeaholics he was deep in denial.

Pretty soon he lost his marriage…his home…his kids…even his dog.

In his lowest moments he even considered writing sad country and western songs.

But he didn't lose all of his friends.

His one remaining mate, a kind soul by the name of George, persuaded him to come round to his house one night for tea.

When Arthur arrived, George welcomed him at the door with a smile. Behind him were his wife, his kids, and his chocolate Labrador (wagging its tail).

The television was on in the background. A programme was just ending. It was one of his favourites. Arthur's nerves began to jump for joy in anticipation of the next episode beginning immediately.

But it didn't.

Instead, he sat through three minutes of adverts. The last one had him in stitches.

Then it had him in tears, as he finally recognised what he had become. How low he had descended.

"You're a Bingeaholic, Arthur," said George, looking sadly at his friend.

That's when I woke up…screaming.

Luckily my screaming woke my wife who recognised the symptoms of my distress, led me downstairs, sat me on the sofa, and switched on the telly.

"Right," she said, handing me my dressing gown. "Now you just sit there and calm down. This programme's nearly finished. Some ads will be on in a minute. Maybe even one of the ones you like."

I put on my dressing gown and looked for my slippers.

"I'll go make you a nice cup of tea," she said.

"Make it Tetley," I said.

It could be epic…it might even be mythic.

So…here's the thing.

Want to know why, these days, streetlights are dimmer, tv programmes are crappier, computers are slower, and beer is flatter?

Want to know why kids are noisier, whites aren't whiter, food is engineered, weather is unpredictable, and coffee is pretentious?

Want to know why reality show 'stars' are moronic, music is forgettable, literature is uninspiring, and humour is serious?

Want to know why peace is violent, death is easy, life is hard, nature is disappearing, and the planet is generally more bloody screwed up than it's ever been?

Here's why…

A distinct lack of unicorns!

Apparently.

If unicorns were around, power would be cheaper and the world would be a brighter, much better place.

Possibly.

Silly old me.

There was I thinking it was about being kind to each other, building a better future, and teaching our kids respect, personal hygiene, cursive writing, reading, silence, and how to develop an eclectic taste in music.

Throw in anything by the Traveling Wilburys, naturally.

Don't get me wrong.

I have absolutely nothing against unicorns.

Far from it. I think they're the dog's bollocks.

Possibly the unicorn's gonads.

I think they're awesome and magical creatures, in a pointy-horned, beautifully mystical kinda way.

Not only that, I think that making them the stars of a cheeky ad campaign for a power company is a pretty damned clever move.

The campaign's mostly about a fantastic new way of producing money-saving electricity.

It's unbelievable.

It could be epic.

It might well be mythic.

It's definitely legendary.

There's even a twist in the tale.

It's all a sendup. Who knew.

I just hope that no unicorns were harmed in the making of the campaign...

The brain that works differently.

People who are creative have brains that work differently.

It's a fact. Well…as near as damn it.

I read about it in an article written by Carolyn Gregoire and Scott Barry Kaufman. [9]

It appeared as a post on Linkedin just after the New Year.

The article tells of a study performed way back in the 1960's, where it was discovered that the creative brain is more primitive…more cultured…more destructive…more constructive…crazier…and saner, than the brain of the average person.

Creative people, said the study, are more introspective and have a greater familiarity with the darker and more uncomfortable parts of themselves.

Interestingly, creative writers score extremely high on all measure of psychological health. These findings probably secretly piss off people who aren't creative but would love to be.

I get it.

It's not fair.

It's like being taken into the best sweet shop in the world when you're a kid…being shown all the goodies…then being told you can't have any of them.

All you can do is look on while kids born with creative brains stuff their faces.

All you can do is stamp your feet, clench your fists, and grind your teeth.

And you begin to imagine all the other things you could do…all the other thoughts you could think…all the other words you could say…if only you had a creative brain.

Then you hear a voice, whispering in your ear.

That's when the penny drops.

You're either creative, or you're not, the voice says.

It's not a matter of choice. It's a matter of grey matter.

A study by scientists at the Cornell University found that creative individuals tend to have a peculiarity in the structure of their brains. [10]

They have a smaller mass of corpus callosum. The cluster of nerve fibres that connect the left and right hemispheres of the brain.

The result? Thinking is less inhibited, more adventurous, and they're more likely to come up with weird and wonderful ideas.

In a stroke of great fortune, this is excellent news for non-creative folk, too.

If you're one of them, you don't have to be inspired…or impulsive…or ingenious…or fantasy oriented…or emotionally sensitive…or wildly imaginative…or quietly innovative…or musically gifted…or whatever.

You don't have to be a writer…or poet…or artist…or singer…or musician…or designer…or actor…or inventor…or photographer…or publisher…or whatever.

It's very liberating.

You can leave all that creative stuff to the folk with a smaller corpus callosum.

While you get on with the important business of making the world a better place.

By doing everything else…

Legends, heroes, and dudes.

There are some people for whom the word 'legend' is entirely appropriate.

They seem to have been with us for as long as we can remember.

They'll still be with us long after they're not around any more.

Even long after we're not around.

They help shape the way we think, sometimes the way we act.

They celebrate the good times with us…and help us make it through the not so good times.

All through a little disc of black vinyl, another one of plastic and aluminium, or a ticket for a live display of bloody musical Bowie magic.

There's another word for people like that.

Heroes.

David Robert Jones was one of the best of them.

Thanks dude.

See you on the flip side…

Ozzy Ozbourne worked in a slaughter house.

There are those who believe that the road we travel along in life is pre-ordained.

They think our fortune, or fate, is decided well in advance. All worked out beforehand.

We have no say in the matter.

We're not in the driving seat.

We might as well sit back and enjoy the ride. Or not.

I have no doubt that the well-meaning folk who believe this do so in the firm conviction that any alternative belief doesn't even merit thinking about.

They know they're 100% right.

Case closed.

They are, of course, 100% wrong.

As a callow, single-figured nipper, I was sure my destiny in life was to be either the next Cliff Richard, a fireman, or the Pope.

Possibly all three.

Then there's Marissa Mayer. Hot CEO of Yahoo. Took pre-med classes at Stanford way before she was Googled. (11) The rest his history.

Apple CEO Tim Cook worked in a paper mill before joining IBM. (12)

Amazon CEO Jeff Bezos worked at McDonalds then ran a summer camp for kids. (13)

Advertising giant Tim Delaney wanted to be a hotel bell hop boy when he left school at 15. (14)

Mick Jagger worked as an ice cream salesman and a porter at a mental hospital. (15)

Douglas Adams was a bodyguard for an entire family of oil tycoons from Qatar. (16)

Ozzy Osbourne worked in a slaughter house. That might explain a lot! (17)

Kurt Vonnegut was the manager of a Saab dealership in Massachusetts. (18)

You see where I'm going here...

Of course there are those who believe that no matter what we start off doing...we end up doing exactly what we were destined to do.

Read my lips.

Bollocks!

Our destiny is to make our own destiny.

Of course not all of us will succeed. Maybe most of us will become nothing but full-scale screw-ups with bags full of lost dreams.

Fate and fortune are real bitches.

Just like my aunt Annie's two ancient Pugs.

Licking your face one minute...biting your ankles the next.

You have two choices.

You can either put up with the licks and the bites and take what life throws at you.

Or you can grab destiny by the throat with one hand...and beat the hell out of it with the other, until it comes round to your way of thinking.

Of course there are some folk who think that it doesn't matter which road you take, you still end up at the same place.

Probably in some slaughterhouse with Ozzy...

May The Force be with you.

The trouble with free speech is that it isn't.
It's nice in theory.
Bloody useless in practice.
And somewhere down the line there's always a price to pay.
The idea that we can say (and do) what we want, and bugger the consequences, simply doesn't work.
Not without the occasional punch-up.
Deep down we know this. Well…most of us.
The reality is that there's always going to be someone, or a whole crowd full of someones, who will be upset by some of our words or actions. Or all of them.
The reality is that there's always going to be something that THEY say or do (or are) that will upset some of us. Or all of us.
The reality is that we can be as inoffensive as a gnat's' fart and there will always be somebody who gets their boxers in a twist.
Case in point.
Something slipped by me at the end of last year.
An ad for the Church of England, featuring people reciting the Lord's Prayer, was due to be screened in cinemas before (or during) the new Star Wars movie.
Not anymore.
It's well made. Great production values. Beautifully filmed. Well cast.
Extremely well-known script. Quite emotional. Touching, even.
Push me and I might say I rather liked it.

But according to some folk (and I include the Digital Cinema Media agency here [19]) it has a flaw the size of Alaska.

Namely…

It would have been seen in glorious, high-definition technicolor…by captive audiences…who might not have appreciated being force-fed 56 seconds of Christian prayer.

With no remote controls. And no fast exit to the toilets.

So it had its plug well and truly pulled.

What's the problem?

I mean…hang on a skinny minute. It's only 56 seconds, dammit.

It's a cinema ad for Heaven's sake. Not a bloody sermon.

It's not violent. It's not rude. It's not full of hate-filled bile.

It's just a lot of people saying a well-known prayer.

Not harming anyone.

Then again…

I remember when our kids were in primary school. The eldest one asked if he could go to a nearby playschool with his friends.

It was attached to a local church.

He was attached to his local friends.

He'd only gone a few times before we had a visit from the vicar, asking us in the nicest possible way when we were going to bring him to church.

Even hang around for the show ourselves.

You'll enjoy it, he said.

No pressure, he said.

We have guitars, he said.

He was on a recruitment drive.

Signing up parents through their children.

Emotional blackmail with a plectrum and a dog collar.

However friendly.

At that precise moment, I was reminded how much I hated anyone trying to stuff their beliefs (no matter what they were) down my throat.

However gently.

I used to be an altar boy. I knew the drill then. I still do now.

I politely declined his invitation. And his loosely veiled advertisement.

In the nicest possible way.

I like my religion the same way I like my ads. There when I need them and nowhere in sight when I don't.

My choice.

Non-disruptive.

Now the path's clear for me to enjoy the new Star Wars movie.

The ultimate epic saga about good versus evil.

Heaven and Hell…in space.

With no praying out loud. Just cheering.

Popcorn by the bucketload.

Giant sized Pepsi.

And a gent's loo in close proximity.

That'll do nicely.

May The Force be with you…

In the nicest possible way...burger off!

Advertising has always had the power to affect the hearts and minds of folk from all walks of life.

Sometimes for the better.

Other times possibly not so much.

With great power comes the threat of great irresponsibility.

And sometimes that irresponsibility involves a pretty nifty exercise in back-tracking.

And eating a large, cold slice of humble pie.

Just like a certain restaurant chain had to do.

There they were, thinking that their new poster campaign, which took a tongue-in-cheek poke at vegetarians, would be the subject of much good-natured banter.

There they were, thinking it was the bee's knees. Or rather the cow's tenderloin.

There they were, thinking that viewers would have the appetite for a little friendly Boeuf Badinage.

And there they were, performing a faster u-turn than a springbok chased by a cheetah in 6th gear across the Kalahari.

All because irate vegetarians and carnivores hit social media in their hundreds...possibly even thousands...to express their profound displeasure.

How dare they.

Didn't they see the humour?

Didn't they get the joke?

Meanwhile, at the Advertising Standards Authority, the phones were going into meltdown.

Well, okay...they were slightly warm.

The restaurant chain wasn't slow to respond.

Not only were they "taken aback" by the reaction (for that, read shitstorm), but they promised to remove some of the ads.

Why just some?

In a statement on its Twitter feed, they said: "The last thing we ever intended to do was offend or alienate vegetarians. The same vegetarians we've looked after since we first opened."

Just for the record...

I'm not a vegetarian.

I'm a confirmed carnivore.

However, I'm also a bit of a munchy herbivore.

And occasionally, I veer towards being a part-time quornivore.

I respect other folks' choice of food.

I expect them to respect mine.

Not take the piss out of it.

However clever and good-natured they think they are when they do it.

So in the nicest possible way…and in the best possible taste…

Burger off!

The boxer and the street fighter.

The last serious punch-up I ever got in the middle of happened few years back.

It took place between my ears.

Just behind my eyes.

My left and right cerebral hemispheres were going at it hammer and tongs.

The logical side (left) is a bit of a boxer.

Good stance. Guard up. Always jabbing with the left. Following up with a solid right cross. Drip drip demolition. Brains not brawn.

The emotional side (right) is a bit of a street fighter.

Visceral. Passionate. Willing to take a solid punch in order to get a better one in. Leads with the heart. Never gives in. Brawn not brains.

I was thinking of buying a new car at the time.

The boxer favoured BMW…or possibly Audi.

The street fighter favoured anything big and meaty, as long as it was black.

The boxer led with the latest hybrid system and an iDrive control interfaced up the wazoo. He had fast hands and nimble feet.

The street fighter ducked to the left and countered with a twin turbocharged engine on steroids, full leather interior, and enough torque to make even the sturdiest crankshaft twist and crap itself.

The fight lasted for months and eventually ended in a draw.

By then the boxer had stopped floating like a Red Admiral and the street fighter had stopped stinging like a white-tailed bumble.

The ref held two tired arms aloft and the crowd went wild.

The thing is…

Everyone has thoughts that follow them like shadows throughout their life.

This is one of mine.

The best, most convincing advertising isn't about either facts or feelings. There is no 'either or'…there's only a bloody great AND.

Undeliable truth AND inescapable emotion.

Somewhere along the line, you end up putting them in the ring together and letting them beat the Hell out of each other until they realise they're just flip sides of the same coin.

I love copy that tells…and copy that sells.

If they're in the same sentence, brilliant.

If they're in the same paragraph, even better.

Just as long as they're in the same damned ad…

The old King might be dead, but the new one is alive and bloody well kicking.

Curious things happen when you sit down at your desk, after the first coffee of the day, to write your next ad.

Without realising it, you get lost.

Truly, madly, deeply lost.

Your sense of time buggers off, leaving your internal clock up the creek without a little hand.

The blood vessels in your lower extremities lose their sense of self-worth.

You lose all emotion in your toes. Starting with the little ones.

Your leg muscles lose all faith in their ability to contribute to society in a meaningful way.

Pretty soon your bladder becomes extremely worried.

Before you know it you've missed your lunch. And every one else's.

Meanwhile, above the waist, closer to the action, all seems hunky dory, as you rattle out heavyweight words of all shape and size on your lightweight MacBook Pro.

And then it's mid-afternoon. You feel a distinct need for caffeine.

So you stand up and take your first steps towards the kitchen. Or anywhere.

And you wonder why your legs feel like they belong to somebody who can't walk properly.

The thing about getting lost in what you're doing is that, by the time you find your way back, you might find that the rest of the world has moved on.

This is a bad thing, right?

Nope. This is a good thing.

This is the time when you grab stagnation by the throat and give it a damned good thrashing.

So what if, just when you learned all the rules, they started teaching new ones.

So what if, just when you knew all the answers, they changed all the questions.

So what if, just when you figured out the language, everything got lost in translation.

So what if you're a stranger in a strange land, and you've just realised that the advertising business you knew so well and loved so much will never be the same again.

So what if it has been taken over by folk who look different, act different, speak different, even think different.

They're young and brave and brash and frighteningly talented…and they're in the process of giving advertising the boot up the backside it's needed for years. Maybe even longer.

Hell, some of them don't even call it advertising any more.

Here's a thought. Extract the digit and get over yourself.

The old King might be dead, but the new one is alive and kicking and bloody up for it.

So read my lips.

You have a choice.

Either smile, grab a desk, grab an idea, and get with the programme…or grab your buckskins, saddle your horse and get the Hell out of Dodge.

I'll choose the former, every day of the week.

Unless the programme's on BBC 3.

With that stupid new bloody logo…

How to become a half-decent copywriter in 30 easy steps.

Becoming a half-decent copywriter (or content writer) isn't as difficult, or as painful, as you might think.

To start with, all you need is a fistful of writing talent, enviable intelligence, and good old common sense.

Then, you merely have to throw in a bucketload of blood, sweat, and tears.

And a healthy dollop of humour, too.

After that, you simply have to find the switch, between your ears, responsible for all those dazzling lightbulb moments.

Whether this switch is a straight off/on, or a dimmer, is up to you.

Then you need to be able to tickle the old qwerty ivories. Whether your ability is of the 'hunt and peck', or the 'touch type' variety, it matters not a jot.

And that's just for starters.

Those are the necessary bits you need tucked up your sleeve, or stuffed up your jumper, before you even get anywhere near the easy bits.

Those are the things without which you might as well go work at B&Q.

Now..these are easy bits. The 30 easy steps.

1. Buy a good pen.
2. Buy a good laptop. Preferably a Mac of some description.
3. Buy an excellent dictionary.
4. Invest in a chair with good lumbar support.
5. Buy a distinctive coffee mug.

6. Don't let anyone else use it.

7. Buy an impressively strong brand of coffee, preferably Java.

8. Make the coffee and let the aroma fill your nostrils. Breathe deeply.

9. Go to your supportive chair and park your arse.

10. Tune out the rest of the world.

11. Read the brief (presuming there is one) thoroughly. Twice.

12. Call the appropriate account handler. Be nice.

13. Ask more questions than you need answers to.

14. Write/type until your fingers bleed. (Blisters are acceptable).

15. Re-write/re-type until they bleed some more.

16. Once the headline's right, take a break.

17. Search for biscuits, preferably chocolate ones.

18. Make more coffee.

19. Move onto the body copy (if required).

20. Repeat steps 14 and 15.

21. Spend extra time on the first sentence and the last sentence.

22. Never regard your call to action as an afterthought.

23. Always read your copy out loud. (Whispering is acceptable).

24. Never be completely satisfied with the end result.

25. Never say these three words: "That will do".

26. Write/type as many, or as few, words as are necessary.

27. Never presume that everyone will love your words.

28. Always make your art director your first (and best) sounding board.

29. Write how you feel, not just how you think.

30. Never write on a full bladder or an empty stomach.

They're the steps, or rather some of them, you need to take if you want to become a half-decent copywriter. Or at least start to.

Easy, right?

But who the Hell wants to settle for half-decent?

What about the folk who are fully-decent? Those who are a damned sight better than decent? Those who are bloody talented bastards? Those with brains the size of a planet. And anyone reaching, or even approaching, the legendary status of writers like Abbott, Brignull, Trott or Henry?

They're the kind of people who inspired so many to get into advertising in the first place.

Me included.

They're the kind of people whose minds could turn thoughts into ideas, ideas into words, words into pictures, and pictures into memories that last a bloody lifetime.

They're the kind of people who could wipe the floor with the rest of us lesser mortals.

Without breaking sweat.

Without breaking wind.

Without thinking twice.

Even in their sleep…

How to be under 30 and over 50 at the same time.

Here's something to exercise your grey matter.

There are over 23.2 million people aged 50 and over, living in the UK. That's over ONE THIRD of the total UK population.

That will rise to around HALF by the year 2020.

In fact, according to the Office for National Statistics, there are now more people in the UK of pensionable age than there are under 16. [20]

And they all buy stuff.

Sometimes expensive stuff.

Now think about this...

According to the Institute of Practitioners in Advertising, the average age of an employee in the ad industry is 34. More than two-fifths are said to be aged 30 or under.

Just 5.3 per cent are 50-plus.

Let that sink in for a second or two.

Just 5.3 per cent.

And they're not all creative.

Now I love young blood.

I love to see the industry awash with energy and enthusiasm and young faces with minimal wrinkles and not a lot of grey hair.

I love to see ideas that are fresh and thinking that isn't suffering from having been reconstituted again…and again…and again.

I love the style, the brashness, the bravado, the invention, the fearlessness, the early mornings and late nights, the work hard play harder ethic, the panics, the pitches…everything that makes under 30's glad they're young and over 50's glad they know how to pace themselves.

But…

I also love to see the industry awash with maturity and experience and memory and safe hands and logical thinking and wrinkled brows with furrows as deep as a ploughed field. And smiles as wide as the bloody Mississippi.

I love the class, the comfort, the judgement calls, the variety, the morning-after nod factor, the excitement of bouncing ideas off someone 20 years younger than you and seeing the look in their eyes that you had in your eyes at their age.

It's a big wide world out there.

And it's full of clients and customers of all shapes, sizes and ages.

If we want to talk to them in a way that makes them want to talk to us…we sure as Hell need to have creatives of all shapes, sizes and ages to match.

Great advertising doesn't care who it happens to.

Or where it comes from…

Don't try to sell it to me...make me want to buy it.

Everyone has pet hates.

One of mine involves reading the words, or listening to the voice, of anyone trying to sell me stuff.

It doesn't matter what it is. How affordable it is. How well made it is. How ingenious it is. Even how damned indispensable it is.

Throw me a sales pitch and watch my eyes glaze over and my interest head for the hills in a well-stocked camper van.

That's why I'm a big fan of copywriting giants like David Abbott, Tony Brignull, Suzy Hendry, and Dave Trott.

To my knowledge, and my great delight, they never tried to sell me anything in their lives.

But by God they made me want to buy stuff.

"Because....." (David Abbott)

"Who said no Englishmen can write a love letter." (Tony Brignull)

"We won't make a drama out of a crisis." (Susie Hendry)

"Lipsmackinthirstquenchinacetastinmotivatingoodbuzzincooltalkinhighwalkinfastlivinevergivincoolfizzin..." (Dave Trott)

The best copy gives me goosebumps.

Makes my intelligence sit up and listen.

Appeals to my emotions.

Tells me stories.

Stops me in my tracks.

Makes me glad I read it.

Makes me wish I'd written it.

The worst copy is banal and predictable.

Unadventurous and drab.

It makes my teeth itch.

It might be full of facts, but it's also empty of everything else.

It tries to take me to places I don't want to go, show me things I don't want to see, and doesn't even apologise for walking in the door without an invite.

I'll never agree with those who think that great copy is merely ink on a page…type on a screen.

And I sure as Hell will never agree with those who think that the only job it has to do is sell.

In 1958, David Ogilvy wrote an eighteen-word headline.

I read it for the first time when I was a teenager. Maybe fifteen or sixteen. It flicked a switch over to the on position somewhere between my ears.

It read: "At 60 miles an hour, the loudest noise in this new Rolls-Royce comes from the electric clock."

Cue goosebumps.

Sure. Good copy might sell.

But…

Great copy makes you want to buy.

Whether you can afford it or not.

Big bloody difference.

To block, or not to block? That is the question.

When I came into Advertising it was still a business of quality over quantity.

At least that's what it looked like to me.

Over the years, the cart very definitely overtook the horse.

Today, it seems, quality has turned into the quiet guy in the back row, and quantity is the arrogant loud-mouthed pain in the arse up front.

It bombards consumers with marketing messages of questionable parentage, and they're all screaming "come on…bloody well look at me!"

Almost everywhere you look. Practically every hour of the day.

No wonder people have had enough.

Particularly web users.

No wonder one in seven British adults is currently using ad blocking software, according to the Internet Advertising Bureau (IAB) UK Ad Blocking Report, conducted by YouGov.

As of June 2015, there were 198 MILLION monthly active users for the major extensions that block ads.

As of October 2015, ad blocking had grown by 41% globally over the previous 12 months.

Then there's Apple.

They created a bit of a stir (as they usually do) a while ago when they announced that their operating system would support ad blocking technology.

Cue hungry cat being introduced to fat pigeons.

The vast majority of websites on the internet exist thanks to online advertising. Millions of them, from tiny blogs to huge corporate-owned magazines, depend on online advertising revenues in order to keep their heads above water.

To make matters worse (or better, depending on your point of view) Samsung supports ad blocking plug-ins for its Android-enabled smartphones.

Some will regard all this as a worrying trend.

A few might even experience the odd panic attack.

One or two may hyperventilate and breathe into the nearest paper bag.

The more enlightened, however, will smile, rub their hands together, and believe it's one Hell of an opportunity.

RAPP USA Chief Creative Officer Frank Iqbal said that, following Apple's decision to become ad blocking friendly, he expects brands to sit up and pay attention.

He added that the onus is now on agencies to improve the quality of their content…and brands to engage with customers in a way that persuades them to come back into the advertising fold.

And therein lies the opportunity.

How we talk to consumers is changing.

What we say to them is changing.

Where we say it is changing.

We can either get with the programme and produce great quality advertising that's more engaging, more relevant, more focused, less intrusive, and less bloody annoying.

Or we can listen to the sound of the room emptying.

Fast…

If it sounds like ad copy, rewrite it.

I've always liked Elmore Leonard.
If you've never read "Get Shorty", buy it.
Don't stop there.
Buy anything with his name on it.
Keep buying.
I particularly like the tail-ender in his Ten Rules of Writing. It goes like this: "Try to leave out the part that readers tend to skip."
Stop a minute or two and just let that one roll across the synapses.
But there's one quote of his that gets me every time. If I could put it on the wall in giant letters over my desk I would. It goes like this: "If it sounds like writing, I rewrite it."
Only I'd change it slightly to read: "If it sounds like ad copy, rewrite it."
Here's why.
Every word of copy I write has to follow one simple rule. It has to sound right when I say it aloud. And I do say it aloud. By myself quietly, or in front of anyone who can't make it out the room fast enough.
It has to sound natural. The way people speak.
It has to have the kind of genuine feel that doesn't get in the damned way of the story I'm telling.
If it sounds like I'm having a conversation with whoever's reading, or whoever's listening, I keep it in.
If it doesn't, I kick it out.
Well, that's the plan.
Sometimes it doesn't work out.

Sometimes ad copy that reads and sounds like ad copy sneaks back in again.

Maybe more often than I'd like. Make that definitely more often.

Nobody's perfect.

Everybody compromises.

That's life.

Then again, sometimes it does work out.

The way I figure it, if I walked into a store and spoke to the guy behind the counter and he answered me back by reading off a prompt card, I'd turn around and reach for the door.

But if he looked me in the eye, smiled, and spoke to me like he was interested in me and I was the most important guy in the store at that moment, I might end up doing something else.

Like reaching for my wallet…

One plus one equals three…or maybe four.

I've always been comfortable with letters.
I feel at home with every member of the alphabet. And as far as I know, they feel at home with me.
Numbers, on the other hand, are a strange brew.
They have always confounded and confused me.
Possibly even bewitched, bothered, and bewildered me.
They're sneaky.
They may conform to certain rules, but I expect that occasionally they enjoy breaking them.
Case in point…
Put me in a creative environment and my ability to perform simple addition immediately goes haywire.
Where the rest of the world believes that one plus one equals two, I somehow come to the conclusion that it equals three.
Sometimes even four or five.
On rare occasions six or seven.
Believe me…I've tried to toe the party line.
I've tried to see the logic of arriving at two. I've even attempted, on numerous occasions, to ignore the threes and fours of life as they try to push their way to the front of my brain.
It never works.
Aristotle was right.
Sort of.

If he was around today and working in advertising, he'd probably shout from the rooftops that one copywriter plus one art director equals a creative team that's greater, and more productive, than the sum of its individual parts.

And it doesn't stop there.

The same thing happens when you shove a copywriter, an art director, a creative director, a Mac operator, and a couple of suits in a room.

Somehow you end up with about nine or ten brains…inside only five or six heads!

Somehow you end up with more ideas than there are walls to put them on.

Collaboration buggers about with accepted mathematical principles and adds extra brains into the equation that just weren't there before.

There may be magic involved.

It makes you think.

When creatives finish collaborating and go back to their separate desks…where does all that extra brainpower go?

It just doesn't add up.

One plus one equals two?

Not on your bloody Nelly…

The art of making human noise.

I had my appendix removed years ago.

It was minutes away from bursting.

I didn't need it before they whipped it out and I haven't missed it since.

It was one of my few remaining vestigial organs.

It used to serve a digestive function way back in the day. Until the day it wasn't needed any more.

I think vocal chords are going the same way.

It might take them a few thousand years to give up the ghost…but the way things are shaping up, we'll wake up one morning and be able to walk the walk.

Just unable to talk the talk.

In 2015, the number of emails sent and received every day was over 205 BILLION. [21]

This is expected to reach over 246 BILLION by the end of 2019.

Here's another jaw-dropper…8 TRILLION (yep, I said TRILLION) text messages are sent every year. That's 350 BILLION every month. [22]

There are currently 5 BILLION mobile subscribers worldwide. [23]

Social networking, which used to be done by word of mouth, is now being done by word of net.

Pretty soon our fingers will be talking more than our vocal chords.

Not long after that our vocal chords will get the message.

"What the Hell have you done for me lately?"

They'll probably get the message by text.

There are some who believe this is progress.

They believe that technology is the new religion and that the future exists at the end of their fingertips.

They walk through life, heads down, thumbs constantly on the move, communicating with the world, ignorant of everything that's going on around them.

They have lost the art of making human noise.

They have given up the sheer joy of speech.

They have banned words to the world of wi-fi.

Don't get me wrong.

I love keyboards, computers, mobiles, internet, social everything, facebook, linkedin, pinterest, twitter, emails, texts, and all that jazz. I love writing at a hundred words a minute…reading at a thousand words an hour. I love silent words, made on a screen. Present when I need them. Absent when I don't.

But I love noisy words more.

Give me the sound of the human voice box.

Give me the joyous sound of infectious laughter.

The heart-rending, gut-wrenching, sound of crying.

The heated sounds of debate and argument.

The soft sounds of love and persuasion.

The excited sounds of surprise and discovery.

The wonderful sound of animated conversation.

All performed with the human voice.

Au naturel.

By default.

Any day of the week…

You gotta love the big green guy.

I admit it.
I'm a sucker for superheroes.
I'm also a sucker for a great TV ad.
I got a twofer this weekend.
Take one of the world's most valuable brands.
Mix it up with the undisputed kings of the superhero universe (and yes, I include the genius known as Stan Lee in there somewhere).
Take a large dollop of super power.
Shove in the greatest sporting show on earth.
Okay, maybe just America then.
Now put them together in a 60-second spot that cost a mere £10 MILLION [24] just for the airtime (we won't even go anywhere near how much the ad cost to produce).
What do you have?
The Hulk versus Ant-Man….all for a sip of new Coke Mini.
Not only did the little black and red guy stick it to the big green guy by stealing his Coke Mini.
Not only did the big guy beat the hell out of a few city blocks to get it back.
Not only did the little guy open the can when big fat fingers didn't have a hope in hell of working the ring pull.
Not only did they end up best buddies.
Sort of.
Not only did it blow every other Super Bowl commercial out of the water and into the next galaxy.
In my humble opinion.

It was the coolest damned superhero and super drink ad ever made. Perfect to celebrate the 50th Super Bowl contest ever played.

Shame I don't understand the bloody game and would rather watch an FA Cup Final.

No matter how good or bad the game is.

Or how crap the commentary is.

Still.

Those yanks sure know how to put on one helluva show.

And you gotta love the big green guy…

Open plan or closed door.

I've worked in cosy creative team offices.

One writer. One art director.

Keep the door open and invite the world to visit.

Or keep the door closed and invite the world to bugger off.

I love the privacy, the quietness, the feeling of personal space, the lack of interruption, the lack of distraction, and the idea that boundaries are there for a reason.

I love the feeling of being part of something small but perfectly formed. The feeling of being in a creative bubble where one plus one equals three. The feeling of being in the team, in the room, in the know.

And I love the feeling of being the flip side of the coin that comes up with the goods.

I've also worked in vast open-plan creative departments.

Group Heads. Writers. Art Directors. Visualisers. Mac Operators.

Uncle Tom Cobley and all.

I love the vibrance, the activity, the multi-layered collaboration, the transparency, the space, and the idea that boundaries don't exist.

I love the feeling of being part of something big. The feeling of being in the game, in the family, in the race.

And I love the feeling of seeing it all happen right there in front of your eyes.

Of the two, I prefer the former.

Although I still get one helluva buzz out of the latter.

I know there's no right or wrong workspace.

I know there's no good or bad workspace.

I know the only space that really matters exists between my ears.

I can walk into an open-plan creative department that's full of noise…full of the buzz…full of the jazz…full of ideas bouncing off the distant walls…and feel like I fit right in.

And yet…

I can walk into a shared office…a creative home…a personal space built for two (or maybe three or four)…knowing that the buzz starts long before I even reach the door.

And it lasts however long I want it to.

And it takes me wherever the hell I want to go.

Inside my head.

Some places make you feel at home the moment you walk in the room.

Others make you feel at home whether you're there or not…

Always sell the sizzle, never just the sausage.

There used to be an unwritten rule when it came to amending creative work.

It was broken down into two parts and went something like this.

Part one: If it's copy…it goes back to the copywriter to re-write.

End of story.

There would be debate. Earnest looks. Maybe raised voices. Possibly something thrown. Occasionally the threat of GBH.

In the end, a compromise would be reached that kept all parties at least reasonably happy.

Part two: If it's a layout, or photography, or typography, or illustration, or style, or anything remotely visual…it goes back to the art director to either amend or oversee.

End of story.

There would be debate. Earnest looks. Maybe raised voices. Possibly something thrown. Occasionally the threat of GBH.

In the end, a compromise would be reached that kept all parties at least reasonably happy.

At some point later, alcohol might be involved.

Life went on.

That was then. This is now.

The trouble with unwritten rules these days is that they just don't make them like they used to.

And some of the ones they do make don't seem to be worth the paper they're not written on.

I have known copy amends made by account executives (even clients) that circumvented writers and went straight to finished art.

I have known visual amends to suffer the same cruel indignity.

The belief (held by what feels like a growing minority) seems to be that anyone who isn't a writer but happens to have a pen can write copy...and anyone who isn't an art director but happens to have a Mac can art direct.

The harsh and sometimes painful truth is that they can.

This is what they tend to do:

(A) Put one relevant word in front of another. Keep going. Stop when they run out of available space. Leave out anything that makes the whole thing worth reading.

Or...

(B) Put relevant images and typefaces together. Add the copy. Stir things around a bit. Stop when they run out of available space. Leave out anything that makes the whole thing worth looking at.

Here's what talented, professional, writers and art directors tend to do:

Their damned job.

The one that gets their juices flowing. And everyone else's.

The one they love doing more than almost anything else they love doing.

The one they can do better than anyone else who isn't either a writer or an art director.

Including amend what they did first, second or, if necessary, third time around.

I think it's time to bring back the old unwritten rules. Including:

The one that says don't buy a dog and bark yourself.

The one that says good enough never is.

The one that says never take credit for somebody else's lightbulb moment.

The one that says always ask for a written copy of every verbal brief.

And my own personal favourite.

The one that says always sell the sizzle, never just the sausage…

Bezos is no bozo.

There's something comforting about Amazon.
Something warm and fuzzy.
If there's been a book published and it's still in print, all I need to do to get it delivered right to my door is go online, order online, and pay online.
Delivery's fast and reliable…and prices are good enough to bite your granny's arm off at the elbow.
I don't need to hunt around the net for any other supplier because Amazon doesn't have a competitor of any significance.
It rules the roost.
It owns the market.
Just like Airbnb, Uber, Twitter, Ebay…to name but a few.
And another thing about those nice folk at Amazon…
They're not bad when it comes to movies, music, games, e-readers, tools, toys, beauty, sports and a whole bloody mountain of other stuff.
In fact, I'd have to be stark raving bonkers to think that this kind of service isn't the best thing since sliced bread.
I'd have to be as mad as a mercury-poisoned hatter to think that Jeff Bezos isn't a bloody genius and a thoroughly top banana, which he probably is.
And yet…and yet…
For me, and this is purely personal, there's something vaguely discomforting about Amazon.
It's the kind of something that whispers: "buy from me because, pretty soon, you won't be able to buy anything like this online from anyone else."

Whether you want to or not.

It's the kind of something that takes your money out of your wallet before you've even thought about taking the damned thing out of your pocket.

The kind of something that says we make more money because we pay less tax.

The kind of something that gives you a choice of one.

I know it's me...not them.

I know I'm more analogue than digital.

I know I shouldn't complain.

Or even feel a teeny bit uneasy.

Despite the tax thing.

That would be small minded and prune faced.

After all, now I know where to go to get what I want when I want it.

No more searching. No more comparing prices. No more queues. No more dealing with 'out of stock' notices.

That's good, right?

No more disappointment. No more waiting. No more birthday or Christmas panics. No more paying over the odds just because the lowest price in town isn't always the lowest price in town.

That's good, right?

Absobloodylutely!

Did I mention the tax thing?

So...why the frown?

Why so serious?

I really don't know...

Maybe I just like a bit of friendly competition.

Maybe I don't like the idea of somebody telling me I don't have a choice.

Maybe it feels a bit too much like the Midlands company that makes ALL the world's supply of Marmite.

Maybe I just don't like all my eggs in one basket.

Maybe I like the feel of print between my fingers.

Maybe I like to browse shelf after shelf of real books so I can discover the gems and touch them and dip in for a quick peek.

Aaaah….good old Jeff has thought of that, too.

He's no bozo.

After playing the harbinger of doom to proper bookstores everywhere (or so some folk would have you believe) Amazon is apparently planning to open bricks and mortar retail stores across the U.S.

The first one opened in Seattle in November 2015. [25]

Divide and conquer, eh, Jeff?

First Washington then the world?

Deja vu all over again?

Clever.

And very sneaky…

Remember number 32.

Life is full of rules and principles. Axioms and self-evident truths. Guidelines and maxims.

It's also full of bullshit and baloney. Hokum and flim-flam. Phooey and poppycock.

These can either guide you over the hurdles and around the pitfalls. Or they can just plain leave you to your own devices and stand on the sidelines pissing themselves laughing.

Some will stick in your memory like a fast-acting dollop of superglue.

Others will disappear into the distance with the wages and the rent money.

Some will make you feel all the better for having known them.

Others will make you feel like you were just in the wrong damned place at the wrong damned time when they came walking by.

There are millions of them.

Everyone has their own favourites.

I have 50 that, for one reason or another, have stayed around long enough to either make me smile and nod my head knowingly, or annoy the hell out of me.

Whether they're true or not is anyone's guess.

My personal favourite is number 32.

Remember number 32 (part two)…

One to ten…
You can't always get what you want.
You won't always get what you need.
Being in love can be the best, and the worst, feeling in the world.
Your children will be brighter than you, get over it.

You'll never be as clever as you think you are, or want to be.

Being drunk is never as much fun as getting drunk.

Getting intelligent is never as much fun as being intelligent.

Dogs will love you whether you want them to or not.

Cats will ignore you unless they want something from you.

You'll never have all the time you need.

Eleven to twenty…

The harder you work the more work your boss will give you.

You'll never be paid what you're worth.

You'll always want to be better looking.

You'll always want to have more money.

Sometimes your kids will hate your guts.

Sometimes you'll hate your own guts.

Overnight success takes years to happen.

School teaches you about learning, not about life.

Money doesn't make the world go around, that's gravity.

Gravity doesn't keep the world going around, that's inertia.

Twenty one to thirty…

The weight of your shoulders is equal to the weight of your troubles.

Marketing isn't the same as advertising.

Just because you can write doesn't mean you're a writer.

Sometimes Death comes before Life, not just after it.

People who are creative have brains that work differently.

This secretly pisses off some people who aren't creative.

Bill Haley never rocked around the clock in his life.

An Art Director isn't the same animal as a Mac operator.

Consumers do read long ad copy if they're interested enough.

Anything worth saying once is worth listening to twice.

Thirty one to forty...

You are not the centre of anyone's universe, including yours.

The greatest writing tool sits between your ears.

The same goes for the greatest art directing tool.

The biggest budgets don't result in the best campaigns.

Some folk go into advertising to win awards...avoid them.

Good enough is never good enough.

Sometimes The Force will be with somebody else...live with it.

Only Glaswegians can say swearwords properly.

Great ideas don't care who they happen to.

There will always be someone better than you...get over it.

Forty one to fifty...

A large Scotch always tastes the same as a small one.

Zombies hate crematoriums.

One plus one sometimes equals three.

Verbal briefs aren't worth the paper they're not written on.

We all begin life as female...this explains a lot.

Light doesn't necessarily travel at the speed of light.

Time only waits for those with a big enough budget.

Clients always want their logo to be bigger.

The average person falls asleep in seven minutes...remember this the next time you present creative work to clients.

The Truth isn't always out there...sometimes it's in here.

I can feel it in my bones.

Back in the day, I knew someone who had a natural affinity with bones.

Her knowledge, and appreciation, of collagen and calcium were beyond the accepted norm.

If there was anything worth feeling that had anything to do with anything, she'd feel it in her skeleton somewhere.

"I can feel it in my bones..." she'd say.

Other folk felt things in their water, or their gut.

Occasionally in their blood.

She felt them in her bones.

It was as if she was digging into the marrow of something deeper and more structurally sound.

Something more solid.

More certain.

More trustworthy.

More experienced.

More knowledgeable.

Feeling it in her bones was how she described a lifetime of experiences, all wrapped up in a judgement call that never seemed to let her down.

I've known some creative directors, art directors and writers like that.

Folk who started life in advertising light hearted (and headed) and got to the point where they were heavy-boned through decades of knowing what to do and what not to do.

Of knowing what to say and what not to say.

Of knowing who the hell could tell their arse from their elbow.

And, just as importantly, who couldn't.

Research from the California Institute of Technology showed that intelligence is something found all across the brain, rather than in one specific region.

It found that, rather than residing in a single structure, intelligence is determined by a network of regions.

All stuffed full of connections.

And another thing...

Being able to make connections between ideas and knowledge may, it seems, help us think more creatively.

As soon as I realised this, I began to see how feeling things in my bones was so much more fascinating than feeling them anywhere else.

Almost.

As soon as I realised this, I began to appreciate how knowledgeable and intelligent the human skeleton is.

How creative it is.

How imaginative it is.

How well connected it is to...well...itself, for starters.

As soon as I realised that, I began to feel something in my bones, too.

And it had nothing to do with osteoporosis...

Verbal briefs aren't worth the paper they're not written on.

I'm not a big fan of verbal briefs. Never have been. Never will be.

They're incomplete.

Inconsistent.

Unprofessional.

Bereft of anything remotely resembling consideration.

Lacking in anything that feels like preparation.

Deprived of large chunks of relevant information.

Even working in tandem, my pen and brain scrabble, and fail miserably, to keep up and fill in the gaps.

The questions I ask are only some of the ones I need to ask. The others show themselves long after the briefing is over.

When I need answers.

I know some creatives who have an uncanny ability to retain information thrown at them in a barrage of verbal facts and figures.

Then make sense of it all.

Clever bastards.

I even envy them.

Unfortunately I have holes in my memory where facts and figures, important or trivial, drip through like honey escaping from a bee-hive sieve.

Rich and golden and succulent.

Give me a well-written brief any time of the day. Any day of the week.

Give me more information than I will ever need. Give me a plethora of relevant knowledge. Give me the low down. The skinny. The inside story. The dope.

Give me page after page of carefully compiled data. Heaps of insights. Clinical evidence by the bucketload.

Give me the chance to browse and discard or digest and use.

Give me everything and leave nothing to chance.

Then leave and let me do the sifting. The arranging. The ignoring. The using now. The sorting away for later.

Let me discover the old hidden gems.

And show them to you, repackaged, in a new light…

Writer's Block? Yeah...right!

Amateurs write when the muse decides to play ball.

Professionals make coffee, hunt down the muse, grab it by the neck with one hand, squeeze tight, then beat the damned thing into submission with the other.

Then they write.

And write.

It doesn't matter whether they're writing a quarter-page press ad, a 60 seconds telly spot, or War and Peace. The process is the same.

They turn over a new page, or stare at a blank screen...then they put one word in front of the other. And keep going.

Doesn't matter what time of day or night it is.

Doesn't matter how long it takes.

Doesn't matter if they're the right words.

Doesn't matter if they're the wrong ones.

All that matters is they're the first words.

The foot soldiers.

The ones who clear the ground. Pave the way. Put up with all the initial shit.

The ones who soak up the first assault on the senses.

Some get sacrificed. Get thrown to the wolves and become collateral damage.

Others dodge the bullets and just keep right on going.

They've earned their place. Their right to stand on their feet when others are on their knees.

They're cannon fodder. Fresh meat for the ancient enemies known as blank space, procrastination and doubt.

Behind them, marching to the beat of their own drum, comes the brigade of born survivors.

Steely-eyed, battle scarred, unshaven heroes, with chewed cigar butts sticking out the side of their mouths.

They know how to get creative.
They know how to get results.
They know how to fight battles.
They know how to win wars.

The stories they tell would make your hair stand on end. Make your pulse race. Make your juices flow. Make you want to walk alongside them as far as you can.

If you can keep up.

Then, when the dust has settled and the final first words have stamped their mark on the page, they're the ones who take five, breathe easy, and wipe the blood off their boots.

After that, they sharpen their wits, refill their ammo belts, adjust their sights, make more coffee, and turn a first draft or a tenth draft into a final one…all without breaking sweat.

Then they do it all over again.
Like every time was the first time.
Writer's block doesn't happen to them.
They happen to writer's block…

The importance of not arriving on time.

I know someone who doesn't know the meaning of being on time.

He doesn't wear a watch.

He doesn't need to.

He's a give-or-take-five-or-ten-minutes kinda guy.

An internal clock kinda guy.

He knows that what he brings to the party when he eventually arrives is much more valuable than most of the stuff others bring when they arrive on time.

Everybody else who knows him knows that, too.

His late arrival doesn't annoy them. It's merely part of his portfolio. It comes with the package. It's in his DNA.

They make allowances. Plan accordingly.

He simply comes up with the goods.

Time…after time…after time…

That's why he gets lots of invitations to work on lots of creative briefs.

And as for those who don't know him…it doesn't take them long to come around to everyone else's way of thinking.

For every one step backwards his fanbase may take, it always travels two, three, or sometimes four steps forward.

He doesn't view creativity as an off-and-on kinda thing. He views it as an always on kinda thing. At least for him.

Even if the front of his brain isn't busy being creative, the back of his brain is. And the sides.

Always.

I read an online article the other day about the difference between creatives who view advertising as merely a job, and those who view it as being paid for something they really love doing.

It struck me that, no matter how much advertising changes (and it sure as HELL has changed)…and no matter how many new words we come up with for old ideas…and no matter how we change the way we talk to consumers, or relate to them, or communicate with them…and no matter how many devices (or apps) we use to make it easier for consumers to talk to the world and get what they want…some things will never change.

People will always want to buy stuff…people will always want to sell stuff…and people will always want to help make it happen.

We're in the help-make-it-happen business.

Doesn't matter how we do it.

Doesn't matter how many people it takes to do it.

Or how few.

Doesn't matter what time of the day or night we do it.

Doesn't matter how much technology we use to do it.

Or how little.

If we just view being a creative as a job…we can arrive at every meeting bang on time…but basically, we're buggered.

Simple as that.

If, however, we view it as something we love doing…passionately and to the best of whatever abilities we have…and we're occasionally ten minutes late because we were busy being passionate about another piece of work…then advertising can change all it bloody well wants.

It won't matter.

What we bring to the party will still be a damned sight more important than what time we arrive…

The difference between hearing...and listening.

Most of the time, advertising is about bringing together people who want to make stuff, people who want to buy stuff, and people who want to sell stuff.

It's about satisfying a need. Making people happy. Making them richer...and poorer. Making them jealous. Giving them the chance to feel better about themselves. Improve their lot. Giving them the chance to spend more than they can afford to. And a million and one other things that, all lumped together, help to make the world go around.

It's business. Pure and simple.

Possibly the biggest, most exciting business in town. And it's very good at what it does.

For most of the time, at least.

But occasionally, advertising steps down off the merry-go-round and does something really tearjerkingly, heartswellingly, worthwhile.

The kind of worthwhile that has nothing whatsoever to do with money.

The kind of worthwhile that has everything to do with making a real and lasting difference to people's lives.

The kind of worthwhile that takes all the consumerism on the face of the earth and, for an all-too-brief moment or two, puts it on the back burner.

That's when advertising becomes so much more than just the sum of all it's varied and incredibly fascinating parts.

That's when it gives its social conscience room to breathe.

The immensely talented, London-based photographer Nadav Kander was commissioned by MullenLowe to shoot a simple yet powerful suicide prevention campaign for the UK organization Samaritans.

The work was funded by Network Rail, to run as posters, in stations across England, Scotland and Wales.

In the UK, jumping under a train accounts for around 3.5% of all suicides. [26] In the UK and ROI there were 6,581 suicides in 2014. [27]

Think about it.

If you haven't seen the posters, you can hopefully catch them on the MullenLowe website, or at adweek.com.

The campaign tagline is: We don't just hear you, we listen."

Take it from someone who listened for many years, this is a campaign worth looking at.

There are far too many that are easy to forget.

It's nice to find one that, for those in need, will be easy to remember...

The Theory of Creative Immortality.

I've often wondered where unused creative ideas go to die.

All those clever thoughts dreamed up in the heat of campaign work or pitchwork.

Put on the wall…then put on the back burner.

All those once-brilliant designs, words, and lightbulb moments that, for one reason or another, dim into insignificance.

Every creative department has a recycle bin for the lucky few.

The ones with potential not yet realised. The ones whose glory days have not yet come. But will.

Born before their time.

Waiting to be eased into the mix next time round in the hope that nobody wearing a suit remembers them from last time round.

But what about the other poor buggers?

The ones who thought they had potential…but didn't.

The ones who could have been contenders…but weren't.

The ones who, like Brando, never got a shot at the title. And now never will.

Where do they go to die?

I think I know.

I think that hidden away somewhere in the darkest jungle of our collective creative minds, there's a graveyard full of the bones of unused creative thoughts.

Stripped of all their strategies and cleverness and logic and imagination and off-the-wall quirkiness.

Lying cold and naked in the darkness.
Unloved. Unwanted. Unhappy.
Waiting…and hoping…
I have a theory.
I call it The Theory of Creative Immortality.
Long story short…
Nothing dies…nothing gets lost…nothing gets wasted…and everything goes into the pot to get reconstituted into something else.
No one gets left behind.
When you think about it…that's exactly what happens to all the molecules and other stuff in our bodies when we bite the dust. Cash in our chips. Take a dirt nap.
We simply reconfigure.
The atoms that used to make up our left earlobe, for instance, might one day make up a tender green shoot that pokes up through the earth at the edge of a beautiful forest.
Or maybe they might be unfortunate enough to make up the part of a politician's brain that governs truth, honesty, and sincerity.
Anyway, The Theory of Creative Immortality says that every old, unused thought or idea somehow gets reconfigured into a new, freshly baked one, ready to use, somewhere down the line.
Sooner or later.
So the next time one of your ideas doesn't make the final cut…don't panic.
One day it will. Or at least part of it.
It might not look the same. It might not feel the same. You might not even recognise it.
But it will recognise you…

Passing The Multiple Nose Test.

I still have the first ad I ever wrote.
It was for a gas powered radio.
I thought the account exec was having a laugh.
I thought it was some sort of initiation ceremony.
I was expecting instructions to roll a trouser leg up, put on a blindfold, and swear allegiance to some hairy-arsed builder with a funny handshake.
What I got was instructions to deliver 150 words (approx.) of glowing copy before end of play that day.
By then it was lunchtime.
It took me half a dozen re-writes to get it right.
Or at least right enough to pass under the nose of a friendly art director, who passed it under the nose of a creative group head.
He passed it under the nose of an Account Director who, at some point, passed it under the nose of a client.
It passed the Multiple Nose Test with low flying colours and was printed in a local paper a few weeks later.
I came across it a month or so back, stuffed in a large manila envelope along with a bunch of other ads and leaflets.
Written by yours truly.
All of which had passed their own Multiple Nose Test at some time or another in the dim and distant past.
A fair amount of literary progress had been made by me between then and now, but it got me thinking.
In the same way that we don't come into this world fully-formed adults, we don't come into this game fully-formed creatives.
We grow. We learn. We make mistakes. A ton of them.

We work our arses off.

Every damned day.

We start our lives in nappies…end our lives in nappies…and somewhere in the middle we do the best damned job in the world.

We work at it until our fingers bleed and our hair turns grey. Or falls out.

It's a wonderful life…but tough as hell.

Hopefully we become better creatives later on in our careers than we were at the beginning.

Hopefully we change at the same rate as the industry itself changes.

Hopefully we help to make that change happen. Despite all of the pain and with all of the joy it entails.

Hopefully we don't waste the time we have, the brains we have, and the talent we have.

Hopefully we always appreciate the magic we create.

Many years ago I came across a quote by a guy called Steuart Henderson Britt. He was born in 1907 and died in 1979. He knew a thing or two about advertising. He said:

"Doing business without advertising is like winking at a girl in the dark. You know what you're doing, but nobody else does."

It's a quote I think every agency should show to every client before they get down to the serious business of working together.

It reminded me about the gas powered radio ad. Reading it again made me realise that keeping it was like winking at a girl in the dark.

I knew what I did, even if nobody else did…

Creativity is contagious...or is it?

Albert Einstein was a damned clever guy.

Curiously enough, although he was widely regarded as a genius, his brain was smaller than that of the average adult.

I like to think that this proves a pretty important point.

Namely, it's not always what you have that makes you special, but what you do with what you have.

Old Albert took his smaller-sized brain and went on a journey that helped to change not only the way we viewed the world...but also the way we viewed the universe.

Relatively speaking.

On the way, he ended up figuring out a thing or two about the way we viewed ourselves.

He came to believe, for instance, that imagination was more important than knowledge.

I agree.

So...up yours, Ben Franklin!

And he said something that barged into my brain and put down roots. Namely:

"Creativity is contagious, pass it on."

Before that, I'd always viewed creativity as a muscle. Not a virus.

The more you use it the stronger it gets. The stronger it gets the faster you think. The faster you think the more thoughts you have. The more thoughts you have the more possibilities open up to you.

The world of advertising has many folk with muscles between their ears.

Mind you, it also has others with nothing but vacant space there.

Anyway…the thought that creativity could be contagious…that you could pass on whatever leaps of imagination you had merely by coming into direct contact with someone else…was almost intoxicating.

The idea that you could communicate a concept merely by touch…from your brain to someone else's, via osmosis through the skin membrane…was like a door opening somewhere inside my skull.

If true, it would have been churlish of me NOT to take full advantage of this exquisite ability.

So I did.

From that moment, I decided to shake the hand of every creative I met.

Vigorously…at great length…and as often as possible.

Whatever creative talents I had (whether I was aware of them or not) I was determined to share with as many people as I could.

Whether they wanted me to, or not.

And by doing so…I would receive in return whatever talents they shared with me. Knowingly or not.

It worked well for a while.

Then something strange happened.

Something unexpected.

Something alarming.

No long after I began my regimen of hand shaking, I noticed that some of my creative colleagues rebuffed my attempts at direct skin on skin contact.

A few retreated to a safe distance. Glaring.

One or two even threatened physical violence if I ever tried to invade their personal space with any of my uninvited palm-on-palm shit.

Maybe they believed their creativity would become more powerful and more effective if they kept it safe inside their skin, instead of letting it seep out through their pores.

Maybe they only wanted to pass on their precious mentoring talents to a select few, as and when they saw fit.

So, reluctantly, I stopped shaking hands. I even put my high fives and fistbumps on hold.

Then something strange happened.

Something unexpected.

Something alarming.

Slowly.

Bit by bit.

I began to feel less creative…

It takes two to tango.

Art Directors are wonderful creatures.

They're sharp…they're seriously talented…(well, some of them)…and they come in all shapes, sizes, and abilities.

There are those who cultivate their own visual side of the fence with consummate expertise…and leave the literary side to folk who know how to get creative with alphabetti spaghetti, but who wouldn't know one pantone reference from the other.

There are those who wear more than one hat…and can do as good a job with words as some writers I've known.

There are those who have more style in one of their little fingertips than many creative folk have in all of their bodily digits combined.

And then there are those highly talented few who seem to be able to combine a whole stack of talents and fit them nicely into one, perfectly formed package.

As someone on the word side of the equation, I've worked with the good, the bad, and the downright ugly. The energetic, the lazy and the couldn't give a damn. The intelligent, the dumb and the brain the size of a planet. The highly artistic, the highly strung, and the highly inebriated.

Occasionally, I've worked with those who had the uncanny knack of making me feel like I found my other half. My better half, sometimes.

And for me, that's what it's all about.

If you're only a yin…you're incomplete.

If you're only a yang…you're unfinished.

You're a one-handed clap.

In the long history of advertising giants, a guy called Leo Burnett stood taller than most. Today, his name is above the door of one of the world's largest agency networks.

So you could say he knew a thing or two about a thing or two.

Here's one of the things he knew better, and earlier, than most.

"Good advertising is a happy wedding of words and pictures, not a contest between them."

I've lost count of the number of art directors I've met who seem to work in a bubble made for one.

Same goes for writers.

It's almost like they are yins, forcibly kept apart from their yang soulmates.

Or vice versa.

God knows how much more creative and productive they could be if only the walls between them came face to face with a man-sized sledge hammer one dark night in a back alley.

Happily, I've also managed to work with some talented art directors who plied their trade outside the bubble.

They're the kind of folk who wouldn't go within spitting distance of anything remotely resembling a bubble made for one if their next paycheck depended on it.

They're the kind of folk who, when it comes to the ad industry's dance with the consumer, instinctively know one particular truth.

It takes two to tango…

Lightbulb moments.

Here's a thought...

Awake, there are times when the human brain can produce enough electricity to power a small, low-wattage lightbulb.

Maybe that's where the phrase "Having a lightbulb moment" comes from.

That instant when the sparks are really flying between the neurons.

That micro-second of sudden realization and enlightenment when the pulse quickens, the eyebrows hitch themselves up, and the penny drops.

If so, then maybe we all have the capacity to be brighter than we think.

To be 100watt instead of just 60.

To be more intelligent than we give ourselves credit for.

Maybe there's even an on/off or a dimmer switch hidden in there somewhere...for when we go to sleep and the neurons take five.

Maybe we all have the potential to be more creative than we realise.

Well...yes...and no.

Sir Ken Robinson, author, highly entertaining speaker, and government advisor on education, is in the blue (yes) corner.

Ken passionately argues that as children we are all naturally creative. However, by the time we grow up, our creativity has been educated out of us.

Wouldn't it be great if we could find a way of keeping it in.

Then in the red (no) corner, we have author and former creative director Gordon Torr, who thinks Ken's argument is a load of old tosh.

In his book Managing Creative People, he says that believing everyone has the capacity to be as creative as the next person is as ludicrous as believing everyone has the capacity to be just as intelligent as the next person.

Gordon passionately believes that creative folk are different from the get go and they stay that way…and that's that!

I'd love to come down on the side of Sir Ken, but I think Gordon has a point. And a pretty damned big one.

It would be nice to think that between everyone's ears is a brain with the capacity to be an artist or a writer…not just a refuse collector or a politician.

But I think it would be nicer to think that every creative department is filled with rebels.

Folk who refused to have creativity educated out of them.

Folk whose grey cells can do things with words and pictures that nobody else can.

That's not to say that only creative folk can be imaginative…can conceptualise…can have ideas. Perish the thought.

I firmly believe that a great idea doesn't care who it happens to.

A lightbulb moment should be free to attach itself to any passing Tom, Dick or Harry…Agnes, Sheila or Liz. But here's the thing:

It should be free to do it again…and again…and again…

It should be free to do it not because it feels like doing it, but because it can't stop itself from doing it.

That's the difference between acting creative and being creative. It's more than just what you do.

It's who you are.

Cradle to grave…

Saving our bacon.

Writers aren't always the best people to check their own copy for typos, misspellings etc.

It's a real pain in the arse…but there's a good reason why.

Make that two.

Ever heard of Saccadic Masking?

Nope?

Me neither.

Saccadic Masking is a defence mechanism. With it, your brain selectively blocks your visual processing whenever you move your eyes.

You can see where your eyes are looking before they start moving. You can see where they end up looking when they stop moving.

But everywhere in between gets blocked out. If it didn't, all you'd see is a constant blur.

And you'd probably feel dizzy and throw up.

The consequence of this is that for about 40 minutes every day there's a gaping hole in your vision.

In effect…you're blind.

In total, for about 10 days a year.

I have a theory.

It concerns the aforementioned Saccadic Masking.

It also concerns an illusion where, when you check your own writing, your brain ignores any missing letters or spelling mistakes.

It trusts your judgement.

It expects to see the complete, correct word, so it skips over the mistake as if everything was hunky dory.

It isn't.

This is where a good proofreader comes in very handy.

One thing you need to understand about proofreaders.

They're not human. They're something….more.

Some folk believe they are what we could be, if we didn't make so many mistakes.

Unlike humans, proofreaders can move their eyes from the first letter of a word (or a sentence, or a paragraph) to the last, normally very quickly, without experiencing any blind spots in between.

They are masters (and mistresses) of Saccadic Masking and Illusion.

They see what we don't.

They don't miss a trick.

Their eyes have exactly the same level of expectation as their brains.

They can spot a misplaced modifier or a misused apostrophe a mile away.

They can tell an Oxford comma from a common or garden one.

Their ability to see the need for an amend knows no bounds.

They are the saviours of many a writer's (and therefore agency's) reputation.

They are neither used often enough nor appreciated often enough.

We mere humans have a lot to thank them for.

They operate quietly in the background.

Correcting our errors.

Saving our bacon…

On the subject of age and creativity.

The subject of age and creativity has reared its cute little head this morning. Not for the first time and undoubtedly not for the last.

It seems, sadly, that there are still folk in advertising's version of La La Land who think that anyone over 50 has no right working in a creative department.

They think that creativity deteriorates not just with time, but also with wrinkles, arthritis, and a need to pee a little more often than usual.

They think that grey hair is a sure sign of rapidly approaching dementia. And that anyone older than middle aged has an inability to come up with a new idea. A fresh thought. An off-the-wall approach.

They have all the sense of a trod-on chip.

Also, sadly, there are still folk who think that anyone under 50 has no right being in charge of a creative department. They think that, when it comes to having a safe pair of hands on the steering wheel, a ton of experience beats the Hell out of enthusiasm and talent any day of the year. And most nights.

In this they might be wrong. Partially.

They think that too many young creatives firmly believe they know it all (or act like they do) and couldn't give a monkey's toss whether you agree with them or not.

In this they might be bloody right.

Thankfully, there are still enough folk in the business who know that the best creativity doesn't give a skinny tinker's cuss who it comes from.

Or where. Or what sex, age, colour, creed, height, or weight they are.

Thankfully, there are still enough folk who know a damned good idea when they see it.

And what to do with it.

The night Santa lost his hat.

I used to have a thing about the fat man in the red suit. No need to deny it any longer. The time has come to fess up. The fact is, I used to think the guy was a little bit cool. Possibly even a large bit.

I think I was about nine or ten.

Sadly, about ten years later, Santa lost his cool.

You know that feeling when you realise the world is changing, and fings ain't wot they used to be?

Well…I saw the fat man in Oxford Street one bloody cold, dark, December evening in London, in 1972. I was 21 and on my way home. He was on his arse. In a shop doorway. Hatless.

It wasn't a pretty sight.

I could be generous and say he was probably using a little medicinal toddy to stave off the brass monkeys weather. I could be mean and say he was drunk as a skunk, with a broken bottle of whisky at his side. Contents buggered and in a puddle by his right leg.

I decided, instead, to be friendly and sympathetic. So I stopped and asked him if he was ok.

He said he was pissed off with the whole damned circus that was Christmas. He said that it was an impossible job, trying to find out if everyone was either naughty or nice. He said he knew they lied anyway, just to get what they wanted for Christmas. He said he hated bloody reindeer.

I asked him what he did for a day job.

He gave me a dirty look and expelled a loud fart.

I fanned the air quickly and said I thought Christmas was a great time of year. The kind of time when folk could be nice to each other. Even if it was only for a day or two.

He started to blubber.

He said that Christmas was just an excuse for folk to get poorer, spending money on stuff that cost too much and nobody wanted in the first place.

I said what about the children?

He said what about them? Kids weren't kids any more. They were just very small consumers with very large expectations.

He said he felt like a fraud. Spreading tidings of comfort and joy to one half of the world, when the other half was right up shit creek. Sans paddle.

I handed him a tissue and said he was being too hard on himself and the world wasn't a perfect place.

He asked me if I'd like a punch on the nose.

Given that he was sat down and probably couldn't get up without help, I thought his expectations outreached his ability, so I politely declined and walked away into the night. A look of sadness on my face.

That was over 40 years ago.

In between then and now I grew up, got married and had children. Of course every Christmas we pretended the fat man in the red suit paid us a visit, and we always gave our sons the best Christmas we could afford.

Then, this year, Santa came back into my life again.

He'd found his hat.

I saw him outside a store in Manchester, one cold, dark, December evening.

Only this time he wasn't drunk, or sprawled in a shop doorway. He was walking slowly up and down, ringing a bell, and greeting everyone who came his way.

He looked old, but his 'ho ho ho' was very effective.

I stopped, smiled, felt an old memory surface, and spoke to him. So…you don't feel like a fraud any more, I said.

He paused for a moment, and then a look of recognition passed across his eyes. Aaaah…the kid who saw me at my worst, he said.

Then he winked at me and slowly pulled a small metal hip flask from one of his giant pockets. Medicinal toddy, he said. Contents intact, he said.

He slid it back out of sight and patted his pocket gently.

We wished each other Merry Christmas…then he started ringing his bell…and I walked away into the night. A look of happiness on my face.

He looked bloody cool…

A real pain in the arse.

I've been a writer for more years than I haven't been one.

I've been a freelance copywriter since about the middle ages. MY middle ages, not THE middle ages. Although sometimes it feels more like the latter rather than the former.

I've been a writer of fiction since Noah built his little row boat. Truth and lies have always been cosy bedfellows and often flip sides of the same coin.

There have been times when putting pen to paper, or fingertip to key, has been as necessary, as automatic, and as easy as breathing.

There have been other times when it has been a monumental effort and a real pain in the arse.

The kind of pain that has nothing to do with hemorrhoids and everything to do with mental saddles.

I climbed back into my old, very worn, western saddle the other day (cerebrally speaking), after my Year of Living Dangerously.

I was hoping it would be as comfortable as the last time I sat in it.

I wasn't entirely disappointed. Eventually.

The creaking cowhide still gave off an odour of ageing friendship.

My mental glutes protested for about an hour or two while my cheeks adjusted. My fingers remained stationary. My screen remained wordless. There was an ache behind my eyes that had nothing to do with looking and everything to do with seeing.

I saw bugger all.

Then my fingers began to move. Slowly at first...then exponentially faster.

My eyes cleared. I saw, heard, and felt my digits pound the keyboard in a manner reminiscent of Joe Lous, the "Brown Bomber", pounding the body of Max Schmeling, non-stop for 2 minutes and 4 seconds, in 1938, before Schmeling's corner threw in the towel. [28] It was round one.

By then, big Max had been knocked on his arse three times.

Around 80 years later, give or take, my fingertips hitting the keys felt a lot like Schmeling's arse must have felt like hitting the canvas.

It hurt like Hell.

But pretty soon, my synapses relaxed, assumed the position, and the pain in my mind's arse subsided to a dull ache.

It hasn't disappeared completely.

Hopefully it never will.

As my old P.E. teacher used to say: "If it doesn't hurt somewhere, son, you're not doing it properly."

I know a man who knows a man.

Dear 2017,

You don't really know me yet, but we'll get to know each other pretty well over the next 12 months.

There may be times when I piss you off. If so, I will always apologise. Maybe not immediately, but definitely eventually.

There may be times when you piss me off. If so, you had better damned well express remorse. A short delay in doing so would be acceptable.

There may be times when my ideas and copywriting are better than okay…but not quite really good. And times when they're better than really good…but not quite bloody great.

Tough shit. It will probably be a wet Monday. I might have a migraine. I'm doing the best I can.

Be patient. Bloody great pops up every now and then. Mostly thanks to all the creatives I'm lucky enough to work with if I get half a chance. Talented bastards.

And if patience isn't your thing…please feel free to eat my shorts.

There may be times when I wish you were called 1980.

It's nothing personal. That was just a very good year. For me anyway.

I have no clue what you've got lined up for me. I don't even know what you've got lined up for yourself.

But I do know this.

If you promise to give it your best shot, then so will I. Barring migraines.

I also know this.

If, for one skinny minute, you don't think that all of us (okay, most of us) are worth every last ounce of your care, effort, imagination, understanding, compassion, respect, and thanks…every damned second of every damned day…then God help you.

Which he probably won't.

I know a man who knows a man who knows 2018 intimately. They've already had a bit of a natter. Over coffee. Your name was mentioned.

The upshot is…you have until December 31st to get your act together and stop the shit from continually hitting the fan.

Screw things up and believe me you're toast. History. Dead Year Walking.

Consider this a friendly heads-up.

Have a nice day.

In fact, have a few hundred.

The woman who thinks she's a chest of drawers.

My nice MacBook Pro informed me this morning that I've had no backups for 72 days.

Rather than getting alarm bells ringing and immediately reaching for my cute little external hard drive, it got me thinking on the whole subject of that other cute little backup...external freelance creatives.

On the one hand, it can be a good thing that ad agencies, of all shapes and sizes, can go without the services of freelance writers and art directors, thinkers and planners, Mac operators and smooth operators for days...weeks...months...years, even.

It shows that whatever they're doing...they're doing it right. Probably.

It shows they've got the talent they need in-house. And it's bloody great. They don't need any backup, thank you very much. Barring the occasional panics and pitches, of course. No unsettling outside influences or interferences upsetting the creative status quo.

Then again...they might be doing it wrong. Possibly.

I read a story recently called The Woman Who Thinks She's A Chest Of Drawers. Okay, I might have written it.

It's about taking things for granted. Things that were once valued now becoming part of the furniture.

Clients do it to their customers. Agencies do it to their clients. Come to think of it, they also do it to their staff. Friends and families do it to each other. In fact, eventually, everybody does it to everybody else.

We can't help it. We're human. It's a familiarity thing. Now and again it breeds contempt. Sometimes it breeds an unsettling desire to yell and give someone a right hook. Other times it breeds a deep and powerful desire to pull digits out of warm, dark, moist places, appreciate what you've got, work like Hell, and pat a few backs.

Every now and then, it breeds the need to open the door and invite a fresh set of eyes in. Or an extra pair of hands. Or another brain. To work with the talented eyes, hands and brains you already have. Just for a while.

After all, a great idea doesn't care who it happens to. Right?

Years ago I came across a bricklayer who was a brilliant headline writer. He was also a brilliant bricklayer, but that's another story.

So...clients, agencies, families, friends...value the people around you. Show them you don't take them for granted. Don't let them feel like a chest of drawers. Or a wardrobe. Or a bedside cabinet. Or a dining table. Or a coffee table.

Appreciate them. They're worth it. Well...most of them.

New blood in old veins.

You know what's so great about kids? They don't give a damn what grown-ups say or think.

Grown-ups hold you back. Tie you down. Screw you up. Follow the rules. Follow the flock. Play safe. They're old when they reach 40.

They've been there. Done that. Got the t-shirt. Ripped the t-shirt. Used it to polish the car. They think they know everything. They're a pain in the ass.

Kids were born with the damned t-shirt on.

They don't second-guess. They don't double think. They don't play by the rules. They don't imagine the consequences. They dream big. They go left when everyone else is going right.

They just do it...like Nike.

You know what's so great about kids in advertising? The same damned thing.

They're new. They're refreshing. They're daring. They're a new broom. They're a breath of fresh air. They're creative. They take risks. They're full of ideas. Often full of shit. They're an injection of new blood into old veins.

They're the future. They were born with the damned t-shirt ripped.

You know what's so great about grown-ups? Don't ask a kid.

Grown-ups are the voice of experience. They know what works and what doesn't. They keep to the track. They don't get lost in the woods. They know what real pain is. They know the cost of all kinds of shit. Physical and emotional.

You know what's so great about grown-ups in advertising? The same damned thing.

They're still cool. Okay...some of them. They're still creative. They're young, in an old kinda way. They always second guess. They always double think. If they can't play by the rules they make up new ones.

They're yesterday. But also today and tomorrow.

They still try like Hell to dream big. The best of them even succeed. They're often full of shit.

They still remember what it's like to be young kids in advertising not giving a shit about anyone over 40. Even though they might be over 50.

Or 60...

Copy supplied by client.

As I said before...I've never agreed with the concept of buying a dog and barking yourself. Sadly, I've known my fair share of folk who do.

The four words: "copy supplied by client" have possibly been responsible for some of the most embarrassing copy the ad world has ever known and cried over. No doubt great clumps of hair have been ripped from once-hirsute scalps.

Maybe that's why there are so many bald (or at least shaven headed) creatives.

Ironically, the very same words have also possibly been responsible for copy that wasn't half bad. Sometimes bloody good.

Maybe that's why there are also so many hairy (and relieved) creatives.

The thing is...those four words generally go hand in hand with three other words.

"Anyone can write."

And it's true. Just ask Jeff Bezos. Just look at the phenomenal growth of self-publishing with folk like Amazon. Bless his little cotton socks. Delivered next day.

Just ask any company that knows its product or service inside out, back to front, and a damned sight better than any agency. And so they should. But do they know how to write about them?

Let me tell you a story.

Many years ago (for argument's sake let's say about 30) a fairly green but reasonably competent copywriter (for argument's sake let's say someone who looked uncannily like me) wrote some copy for a full-page press ad.

The copy chief liked the copy. The Creative Director like the copy. The Account Handler liked the copy. The client loved the copy.

However he loved his wife more...and when he showed it to her (she always wanted to be a writer) she pulled a face and persuaded him to let her have a go.

The result, delivered back to the creative department by a sheepish Account Handler, was somewhere in between War and Peace and something the neighbour's dog extruded on the opposite side of the fence.

There was a post-it note attached to the text. It said: "Copy supplied by client". The implication was obvious.

The writer had a word with the copy chief...who had a word with the Creative Director...who had a word with the MD...who promptly tore the Account Handler a new one.

It wasn't a pretty sight.

Then he picked up the phone. He was very polite. But he was very persuasive.

Three weeks later the ad appeared in a national newspaper. Copy supplied by agency.

When the client saw how well the ad performed, he sent the writer a case of wine. By way of an apology.

Naturally it got sidetracked.

When, six months later, the client and the agency parted company (for argument's sake let's say amicably) the agency MD sent the client an email. It consisted of one sentence. Seven words.

"Never buy a dog and bark yourself."

When I write my ears don't work.

I come from a musical family. Sort of.

When I was growing up, folk with the same surname, living in the same village, always seemed to be either playing something...singing something...or listening to something on the radio or record player.

More often than not the playing of instruments and the singing happened at the same time. Particularly if there was a little alcohol involved. And the more of us there were, the merrier it was.

Sound was important to us. Music was essential. We weren't quiet people.

So it came as a bit of a shock to the system to discover that when I began writing for a living, my ears didn't work.

Physically there wasn't anything wrong with them. They had all the necessary bits in all the necessary places.

They simply refused to let sound in as long as I had a pen in my hand or a keyboard at my fingertips. They slammed the door firmly shut on any incoming noise. Music. Conversation. The peripheral interruptions of the world.Banished.

It reminded me of that Spartan fella King Leonidas and his 300 warriors (plus associated mates) at the battle of Thermopylae.

Personally I believe the Spartans had ears that refused to work, also. They had all the necessary bits in all the necessary places. Their ears simply refused to let the sound of the dying enter their external acoustic meatus as long as their attached bodies had swords and spears in their hands and breath in their lungs.

Hence the ensuing silence allowed them to concentrate on the business of being David to the Persians' Goliath, and they put up one helluva fight against a vastly superior force.

Their loss was Greece's gain.

Actually, there is some evidence (as yet unsubstantiated) that the reason the Persians were victorious had nothing to do with their phenomenally greater numbers, and everything to do with the fact that their ears didn't work either.

That nice fella Herodotus may, or may not, have had something to do with that. The evidence, not the ears.

Anyway...since then, ears everywhere have had two choices.

One. Work properly and let the rest of the world in to disrupt or inspire their thinking and acting. Or...

Two. Refuse to work and let folk attached to them enjoy the blessed sound of silence.

Ever since the first time I picked up a pen (or crayon), my own ears have preferred the latter.

I'm sure millions of damned fine writers prefer the former. Whatever works for them.

Not for me the hips of Elvis or the crooning of Old Blue Eyes to set the mood. Not for me the orchestral manoeuvres of Johann Sebastian or Wolfgang Amadeus to lift the spirits (and the quality of my copy). Not for me the cavortings of John, Paul, Keef and Mick, or the pure poetry of little Bobby Zimmerman to drive my paragraphs forward.

I like Paul and Art.
I like the sound of silence.
Until the pen goes down.
Until the fingers come off the keyboard.
Then the eardrums open the acoustic doors.
Then the world comes rushing back in again.
Then all bets are off...

Does my name look big enough in this?

To some clients size is everything.
Whatever product they make.
Whatever service they offer.
It's only natural that they want it to be bigger...better...louder...more powerful...more advanced...more popular...better looking...and more memorable, than anything anyone else can make or offer.
So when it comes to advertising what they make or what they do, it's only natural that they think the bigger their name or logo is...on the page or on the screen...the more successful their product or service will be.
And it's only natural that they expect their agency to shut the Hell up and make the damned thing look like it's been force-fed steroids.
They have an almost primitive fear of small.
It makes them nervous.
It makes them feel diminished.
It makes them over compensate.
Picture the scene...
Client: I LOVE this ad. Love it!!
Agency: You do? Fantastic!
Client: Absolutely. It's the dog's bollocks!
Agency: Brilliant.
Client: Only one thing...
Agency: Um...okay...
Client: The logo.
Agency: Too big?
Client: Too small.

Agency: Really? It's already big. How much bigger were you thinking?
Client: There's a lot of space. Couldn't it go there?
Agency: But...but...that's for the copy...and the design.
Client: How much am I paying for this?
Agency: I'll get it redone by tomorrow. Okay?
Client: Peachy. Oh...and about that typeface...

(Later...back at the Agency)
Creative Director: Bad news guys. He likes the headline...
Writer: Bollocks! Body copy cut?
Creative Director: 'Fraid so. And MUCH BIGGER logo.
Art Director: Shit. Is he that small guy with the big car?

Flip sides of the same coin.

There was a time, in the dim and distant past, when I had a notion of becoming a commercial artist.

Remember them?

They looked so cool.

So imaginative.

And so bloody gifted.

Better still, they worked in advertising.

In creative departments.

And they even changed their name to art directors.

Talented bastards.

They were a breed apart. And I was jealous as Hell.

I told my long-suffering art teach about my plan to go to art college and one day step through the door into the glamorous world of ad agencies.

He nearly pissed himself laughing.

I had, he informed me scathingly, about as much chance of making the grade as a commercial artist as Henri de Toulouse-Lautrec had in 1864 of growing taller than 5 ft. 1ins.

Que sera sera...

"But you're a half-decent writer," he said. "If you want to work in advertising so badly, why don't you let somebody else (meaning somebody with artistic talent) worry about the pictures...and you can take care of the words?"

There are times when life hands you lightbulb moments.

You can choose to ignore them, fumble around in the dark, and continue beating your head against the nearest metaphorical brick wall.

Definitely causing untold pain and disfigurement. Possibly needing emotional plastic surgery.

Or you can flick a switch, shine a light on a million possibilities, and avoid compound fractures of the mind, the heart, and the soul.

I chose the latter.

The first time I was teamed up with an art director (a junior one, and female), it felt like I had found something that, until that moment, I didn't realise was even missing.

I discovered that the pair of us together added up to more than the sum of our individual efforts.

Good old Aristotle.

And I also discovered what happens when you cross-fertilise talent.

Most of the time I came up with the words. But sometimes she did. Most of the time she came up with the visual ideas. But sometimes I did.

We were flip sides of the same coin.

We were two 20p pieces of creative currency that, together, added up to 50p.

One plus one really did equal three.

It's been that way with most of the art directors I've worked with.

I've been lucky.

But change has a habit of creeping up behind you and biting you on the arse.

A few years ago, technology gave us a new breed of creatives. Digital wunderkids who can stand on their own feet (or rather sit at their own Mac) and pull together words and images that sometimes make clients go weak at the knees.

Talented bastards.

Maybe (as some folk thought) the old teamwork of half writer/half art director has had its day and needs to be kicked into touch to make way for the new generation teamwork of half mac/half human.

Or maybe...just maybe...(as other folk, including me, thought) we should give more credit to the third option.

The one that belongs in The Department of Stunningly Bleeding Obvious.

The one that joins up the best minds. Produces the best work. Doesn't give a damn which of them comes up with the best ideas.

The one that takes past, present, and future...words, art, and technology...blood, sweat, and tears...shoves them in a room together...and cracks open the beers when they come up with something absolutely pure bloody magic.

The trilogy. The triptych. The trinity. (No doubt unholy)

The glorious equal partnership of writer/art director/digital wunderkind. Each with their own mad skills. Each complementing the skills of the other.

Our Physicists tell us there's no such thing as a three sided coin. Not in this universe.

Our Accountants tell us that 20p, plus 20p, plus 20p, doesn't have a cat in Hell's chance of adding up to £1.

Our Magicians tell us that anything's possible...just don't forget the damned beers.

Why art directors don't snore.

Picture the scene...
It's Friday.
Outside, it's cold, dark, and damp.
Inside, the clock on the wall of the city-centre ad agency's creative department says 4.29am.
In a small, glass-walled, corner office, a single anglepoise lamp is shining a lonely light on a desk awash with A3 sheets of paper.
Scribbled images and scrawled words are on the sheets.
At the desk, two individuals are fast asleep. They're both wearing t-shirts and faded jeans. One has a shaved head. The other has a pierced left earlobe.
Their shoes are off.
Their heads are resting on the desktop on bent arms.
Their minds are resting after working non-stop through the night.
Their deadline is Friday lunch.
One of them is snoring.
The writer.
Outside, a few drunken shouts and the bark of an urban dog fox are the only sounds that interrupt the silence.
At 4.30am precisely, from somewhere under the papers on the desk, the alarm on a smartphone belonging to the younger of the two individuals...the art director...comes to life.
The noise, blasting out a rock guitar riff at full volume, causes the physical state of both individuals to change from fully asleep to fully awake.
The change happens fast.

Roughly a quarter of a second, start to finish. Give or take.

Not a pretty sight.

The writer, scrabbling to find the phone and kill the alarm, is the first to speak.

"Bollocks...I'm getting too damned old for this shit," he groans, wiping drool from the side of his mouth. "Did we crack it?"

"I think we might have dented it," says the art director, standing up, yawning, and scratching an itch south of the border. "I need a pee and a coffee, in that order."

"The last time I pulled an all-nighter was about 10 years ago," says the writer.

"I thought the last time you pulled an all-nighter was a blonde pole dancer two weeks ago."

The writer blushes at the memory, then frowns. "Hang on a skinny minute," he says, looking at a single headline scrawled in black on a sheet sitting at the top of the pile. "I didn't write this."

"Very true, Sherlock. I did," says the art director. "It's a bit off the wall, I know...but around three this morning I swapped roles and had one of your David Abbott moments."

"Bastard," says the writer, grinning all over his face. "It's bloody brilliant."

"Yeah...you were snoring your arse off."

The writer can feel his creative juices begin to flow. "Remind me to snore my arse off more often. This is well and truly cracked. Now all we need is an image," he says, slapping the desk.

"Your turn, mate. Feel free to have one of my John Hegarty moments," says the art director, enjoying another southerly scratch and heading for the gents before heading for the kitchen.

Liquid out. Liquid in.

Outside, right on cue, the dog fox barks again...

Where magic happens...

The secret life of Comfort Zones.

Let me tell you a story...
Comfort Zones aren't what you think they are.
Not by a long shot.
You'd think that they'd do everything they could to make sure that everyone on the inside is shielded from the cares and woes normally experienced by everyone on the outside.
And they do.
You'd think that they'd do everything they could to make sure that everyone in every Zone is chilled out and stress-free. With anxiety in neutral and the engine switched off.
And they do.
You'd think that they're the epitome of calm, rational, self-control. Rock steady on the outside...and a damned sight more of the same on the inside. Right?
Not on your Nelly, buster.
Secretly, under the surface, every Comfort Zone is a mass of quivering neuroses.
A twitching blob of rampant paranoia.
All they want to do is take away the bad shit, and keep you safe.
All they want to do is leave you with the good shit, and keep you happy.
That's why the moment you enter a Comfort Zone, it acts like a giant psychological sponge. Soaking up all your fears, anxieties, concerns, doubts, forebodings, horrors and screaming abdabs.

Leaving you free to breathe. Unwind. Calm down. Lighten up. And feel more safe. More confident. More self-assured.

Instead of being a nervous, jibbering wreck, curled up in a foetal position in a dark corner somewhere. Waiting for the next panic attack.

And it pays a heavy price.

A Comfort Zone, if it is to be successful, needs to sacrifice itself.

Without a second's hesitation.

Without thinking of the consequences of its actions. Or its own wellbeing.

It needs to step up to the plate. Be an unsung hero.

Hurting. Bruised and bleeding. But still standing tall and proud.

The guy who saves the day but whose face or name nobody can quite remember.

And yet...and yet...(and here's where the real secret lies)...

A Comfort Zone also needs to be the guy who kicks your arse out the door.

Away from the protection of the emotional sanctuary.

Away from the safety of the cerebral gated community.

Out to where the risks are.

Out to where the danger lies waiting.

Out to where you're naked and vulnerable.

Because that's where the unpredictable happens. That's where renegade thoughts come jumping off the wall. Where new ideas come bouncing in from left field.

Where creativity and imagination are waiting to poke you with large pointy sticks.

Where a lack of comfort goes hand in hand with a surplus of courage.

Where lightbulb moments come into the world kicking and screaming.

And where magic always happens when you least expect it...

The tools of the trade.

According to the Electronic Textbook of Hand Surgery, you'll use 29 bones, 29 joints,123 ligaments and 34 muscles...just to type this single sentence.

Doesn't matter what the sentence says. Doesn't matter how long it takes to type it. Doesn't matter what kind of typewriter you use.

As long as you can touch type, using all the fingers and thumbs at your disposal, the numbers, apparently, stay the same.

29...29...123...34.

Doesn't matter if your name is George Orwell, the novel is Nineteen Eighty Four, and the sentence is: "It was a bright cold day in April, and the clocks were striking thirteen."

Doesn't matter if your name is J.D. Salinger, the novel is The Catcher In The Rye, and the sentence is: "If you really want to hear about it, the first thing you'll probably want to know is where I was born, and what my lousy childhood was like, and how my parents were occupied and all before they had me, and all that David Copperfield kind of crap, but I don't feel like going into it, if you want to know the truth."

Doesn't matter if your name is David Ogilvy, the client is Rolls-Royce, and the sentence is: "At 60 miles an hour the loudest noise in this new Rolls-Royce comes from the electric clock."

It takes the same number of bones, joints, ligaments, and muscles to write the best sentence you've ever written. Or the worst.

The difference happens up top.

Up in the rarefied atmosphere between your ears.

Where around 100 billion nerves and trillions of synapses spend their entire lives helping you to put one thought in front of another without tripping up or falling down.

They don't give a damn how long or short your sentences are.

They couldn't give a toss whether the words you use are highly memorable or instantly forgettable.

That's up to you.

Their job is to make sure that, when you put gas in the tank, switch on the engine, and slip into gear...they're ready and willing to take you wherever the Hell you want to go.

If you're up for it.

Helped not just by letters...but also by numbers.

29...29...123...34.

Five 'Beetles' called Helmut, Julian, Ned, Max, and Bill.

Here's what I think...
The manufacturing, selling, and marketing industries were formed and built on one simple premise.
Three small words.
Billions of possibilities.
Folk need stuff.
They always have done. They always will do.
Doesn't always matter what the stuff is.
Doesn't always matter how much it costs.
If somebody makes it...somebody will want to sell it.
Then somebody will want to buy it.
Then somebody will want to sell it for less.
Then it's war.
Then more folk will want to buy it.
Even if they can't afford it.
It's a supply and demand thing.
Then in 1959 it became a creative thing.
An advertising thing.
Mostly thanks to five men.
Their names were: Helmut Krone, Julian Koenig, Ned Doyle, Maxwell Dane, and Bill Bernbach.
The original 'Beetles'.
The first two came up with what's largely thought of as the best advertising campaign of the 20th century.
The other three, ten years earlier, founded the advertising agency that made it possible.
The agency was DDB. And they had a thought.
It was this:

"Let's stop talking at people and instead start conversations that lead to action and mutual benefit." [29]

So they introduced a new approach that relied on insight into human nature, respect for the consumer, and the power of creativity.

One of the results was the groundbreaking "Think Small" campaign for their client Volkswagen.

For a car called a 'Beetle' that was initially designed in Germany during World War II.

The campaign, like the vehicle, was a masterpiece of minimalism.

And a whole lot more.

It didn't just sell lots of cars...it sold lots of lifestyle.

And it made advertising damned cool.

Look up the ads sometime. In fact print them out and hang them on the wall.

And the next time you pick up a pad...or a pen...or a keyboard...and you want to create something powerful and memorable (and maybe even off the wall), remember where (and when) creativity in advertising was born.

Remember Helmut, Julian, Ned, Max and Bill.

Advertising's very own 'Beetles'.

Because when you want to be huge, sometimes it pays to think small...

Hearts, souls and Bengal tigers.

I am a dedicated fan of the old and the new.
Always have been. Always will be.
I love old heads on young shoulders. And young heads on old ones.
I love my creativity raw and dirty, with a pad and a pen.
I love it smooth and clean, with a Mac and a keyboard.
I love big ideas and small Southern Comforts. Thinking that makes my skin tingle and my heart skip a beat.
I love talking to folk who think there's nothing left that hasn't been said, shown, or done before. And I love the idea of proving them wrong without feeling the need to rub it in just to prove the point.
I love working with art directors who surprise the Hell out of me by coming up with headlines I wish I'd thought of. Then coming up with images I could never think of in a million years.
I love digital designers who can bring a screen to stunning life and weave their silicon magic into the space between two pixels.
I love clients who love their products so much they're prepared to trust their future to people who love advertising just as much.
I love suits who were taught how to present to clients properly (even if that means knowing when to shut up and let the work speak for itself).

I love suits who instinctively know (and accept) that the folk in the creative department aren't just very cool and sometimes very annoying...they're also the heart and soul of the agency.

I love creatives who instinctively know that suits are the V8 engine under the hood that makes the damned car purr like a Bengal tiger and move like greased lightning.

From zero to hero in the blink of an eye. Or however long it takes.

I love passion.

For the business. For the work. For the people.

Passion in every letter of every word of every sentence of every paragraph of every piece of copy that somebody somewhere reads at least twice.

In every pixel of every photograph and every penstroke of every layout of every ad (in every medium) that somebody somewhere is captivated by at least twice.

Because once simply isn't enough.

Never has been. Never will be...

The call centre guy named Brandon.

I have no problem with call centres.

I know they perform a valuable service.

I have no problem with them being based in India. Or anywhere else in the world, for that matter.

I'm an equal opportunities call centre customer.

I'm sure the people they employ work very hard. I've no doubt they're very helpful, do a great job, and most likely get paid a pittance compared to anyone in the West doing the same job.

They're just trying to get by. Just trying to earn a living. Just like the rest of us.

I have no problem with their excellent telephone manners or their accents. I can understand some of them a damned sight better than I can some of my own countrymen.

Whatever time they call.

The problem I have is with their names.

Not their real ones.

I'm talking about their cosmetically altered ones.

Their pretend ones.

Their Westernised ones.

I had a call from someone yesterday. Very polite. Very friendly. Very respectful. Very enthusiastic. Very Indian sounding.

He told me his name was Brandon.

BRANDON?

Oh give me a break!

The conversation went something like this:

Me: Your name's Brandon?

Him: Yes sir.

Me: Honestly?

Him: Yes sir.

Me: What's your real name?

Him: Brandon.

Me: I spoke to one of your colleagues yesterday. He was very nice. I think his name was Oliver.

Him: I don't know him, sir. I'd like to ask you a few questions. I promise I'm not selling anything and I'll be very quick.

Me: Okay. Tell you what. You tell me your real name and I'll answer all your questions.

Brandon terminated the call.

Maybe he went to have a coffee break with Oliver. The one he didn't know.

Here's a thought.

For the attention of all the companies in the West who outsource their service calls to very helpful, hard-working people in the East.

CHANGE YOUR SCRIPTS!!

I don't need to know the name of the person who's talking to me. I might not be able to pronounce his or her name anyway. It's not important. They might not be able to pronounce mine. I don't mind not knowing. It's no big deal.

What I do mind is the belief that just because you give a Westernised first name to somebody who doesn't have one...I will automatically feel more comfortable talking to them.

Wrong.

I realise there's probably a highly qualified psychologist somewhere who believes that this is a good idea. That I might think the "real" names of overseas call centre employees are too foreign and unpronounceable.

That trying to say them will make me feel uncomfortable. Or even embarrassed.

Trust me. It won't.

That kind of thinking just pisses me off.

I'd be much more inclined to talk to them if they were honest with me. If they told me their real name (or just left it out unless I asked for it), told me which organisation or company they were speaking on behalf of, and asked me if I could please answer a few simple questions.

Then I wouldn't be pissed off.

Then I wouldn't find an excuse not to talk to them.

I might even be interested.

I might even say yes, they can ask as many questions as they want.

I might even engage in a little friendly banter.

But if they call themselves Brandon? Or Oliver?

Sorry.

Have to go.

Someone's at the door...

Space, privacy, and a kick in the nuts.

Years ago, I remember having an extended discussion, in a nearby bar, with my then new art director partner.

The topic? What makes up the ideal creative department.

It was accompanied by much imbibing of alcohol. Some of it of the barley mash variety.

Our opinions differed. As opinions should in all good discussions.

We had one rule.

No reputation of any writer, visualiser, illustrator, art director, creative director, or junior anything, should be harmed during the making of the entire conversation.

We were talking about important stuff.

Bricks and mortar. Layout and decor. Space and ergonomics. Glass and wood. Metal and plastic. Furniture and paint.

All pros and cons were given a damned good going over.

In the end, it came down to size.

What worked best? What gave creativity the perfect environment to flex its muscles?

Big open spaces? Or small enclosed ones?

I came down on the side of cosy dedicated offices for writer/art director teams.

Nice and private.

He came down on the side of knocking down walls and creating one large, open plan expanse.

Nice and public.

Part way through, we were joined by an annoying suit who thought that creative departments were changing.

"They're evolving," he said. "Seriously...ten years from now you won't recognise them," he said.

Already I was seriously thinking about giving him a swift kick in the nuts.

"We did the theory of evolution last night," said my art director. Ever the peacemaker.

"Yeah...tonight we're talking about the theory of size," I said. "Physical dimensions and accessories."

"Size isn't everything," said the suit.

"Tell that to your girlfriend," said my art director.

The suit blushed and left hastily in the general direction of the loo.

Rearranging his nuts as he went.

While he was away, we decided that, every time it was his round, we would order doubles of something suitably expensive.

Back on topic, I reminded my art director that the sadly and dearly departed Mister Cool of the advertising world, otherwise known as David Abbott, once said he could never work in an open plan creative department.

He preferred an office. Even though he kept the door open most of the time.

Good enough for him...good enough for me, I said.

My art director said offices were fine, as long as they were for unimportant things. Like meetings. And briefings. And pitches. And storage. And hiding away.

The real work was done in plain view of one's peers, he said.

He told me that Abbott also said there were plenty of brilliant copywriters who loved a hefty bit of elbow room. And leg room. And arm room. And belly room. And head room. And every other kind of room, as long as wasn't split into small offices.

At least that's what he thought Abbott said. Or maybe that's what he thought Abbott meant.

Sadly, the great man wasn't around any more to argue the toss.

The suit returned from draining and probably examining in detail his allegedly miniature Anaconda. He belched loudly and took our orders.

Two large peaty somethings from North of the Border, we said.

He went to the bar.

My art director finished the dregs of his pint. I like the idea of a big room for big ideas, he said. Lots of background music. Lots of banter. Lots of inspiring stuff.

I said that sounded like lots of noise.

He said that noise was nectar for the creative mind. Or it might be ambrosia.

I said so was peace and bloody quiet.

I made a mental note to use that noise and nectar line somewhere.

The suit, who by then was back from the bar with three very large peaty contributions to the party, smiled.

It was the kind of smile performed by someone who has just thought of something damned clever to bring to a conversation.

"Want to know what I think?" he said, taking a small sip of his large peaty something.

"Only if you buy the next two rounds," said my art director, who, as well as liking a bit of space in his life, also liked a bit of life in his space.

The night was still young.

The suit was still annoying.

Plenty of time to perform a well-aimed kick in the nuts...

Don't drop the bloody baton.

According to Olympic rules, the relay baton should be a smooth, hollow, one-piece tube made of wood, metal or any other rigid material.

It should measure between 28-30 centimeters long, and between 12-13 centimeters in circumference. [30]

It must weigh at least 50 grams.

The first thing you need to do with it in any relay race is grab it and hold on for dear life.

The last thing you need to do with it is drop it.

Ask the two Darrens, Braithwaite and Campbell. Olympic 4x400 relay team members in Atlanta 1996.

There was Campbell...crouched like a powerful coiled spring waiting to be released during the third heat...

There was Braithwaite...sprinting towards him like the clappers to hand over the baton...

There was the baton...falling through the air as it was fumbled and dropped.

Team GB, as it came to be known three years later, was disqualified from the race.

The harsh truth is...it doesn't matter how good you are (or could be)...if the baton doesn't get passed on (for whatever reason), everything goes pear shaped.

Everybody in the ad business (or every business, for that matter) has a baton to pass on.

In most cases, it's not small, cylindrical and lightweight.

It's large, of indeterminate shape, and potentially career-changing.

It's called experience.

Over the years, I've known plenty of grey-haired creatives (and many not so grey) who have been more than happy to pass on what they've learned to the green, crass, loud, shy, and talented young bloods coming up behind them.

It's easy to see why.

They were giving something back to a business that had helped them do so much in their lives. Apart from just survive.

Like pay the mortgage. Buy the car. Put their kids through school. Put food on the table. Pay for more than a few holidays.

Pay for more elective plastic surgery.

But more importantly...it allowed them to do something they actually loved doing. Something they were often passionate about.

And when the time came to pass the baton on to the new kids on the block, they didn't fumble. They didn't drop anything. They didn't think twice. They just did it.

They gave up their time. Shared their experience. And helped turn kids with less experience into men and women with more experience.

But... over the years, I've also known plenty of grey-haired creatives (and many not so grey) who have been less than enthusiastic about passing on what they've learned.

They were small minded.

Still are.

Couldn't see the bigger picture.

Still can't.

Wanted to keep all that experience to themselves.

Still do.

Wanted to leave it up to somebody else to pass on the baton.

Still do.

Wanted to look after number one. Not realising that by thinking like that, they put themselves a million miles away from actually being number one.

So...when the time comes to grab your particular baton, and pass it on to the next guy (or girl) in the race...hold it tight, run like Hell, don't hesitate, don't fumble, hand it over without dropping it...and give them a better chance to run with what they've got and be better at what they do.

Even if nobody did that for you...

The coolest damned horse in the race.

Once upon a time…
People in creative departments had power.
Real power.
Top of the heap power.
We were clever buggers.
We still are. And cool.
We held the keys that unlocked the doors that led to the magic kingdom.
We still do.
Through the ingenuity of our imagination we could create worlds where wishes came true and dreams were things you could actually reach out and touch. And hold. And own.
We still can.
We were the people who entertained you. Informed you. Taught you. Impressed you. Convinced you. Surprised you. Comforted you. Delighted you. Reassured you. Excited you. Empowered you.
Helped you think big.
Helped you think small.
Helped you laugh till it hurt.
Helped you cry till it hurt more.
We were the people who gave you ideas that made the hairs on the back of your neck stand up.
We still are.
We were the people who helped you see that impossible was just another name for something we hadn't figured out yet.

We were also the people who promised to let you know when we finally did figure it out.

And then we became the people who know that time never stands still.

Things change.

What worked yesterday, probably won't work tomorrow.

What we used to say in the past isn't what we need to say in the future.

We realised that there's more than one way into the magic kingdom.

More than one way to make wishes and dreams come true.

And it doesn't take place inside any creative department.

It takes place through the connecting door.

Where data and analytics, click rates and churn rates, closed loops and conversion paths, customer relationship management, social media, search engine optimization...and a hundred and one other cool technologies are lining up to help run the show.

Sometimes behind us. Sometimes in front.

Where a different kind of magic lives.

Where the science of Marketing is just as important as the art of advertising.

Once upon a time people in creative departments had power.

Real power.

We still do.

We might not be the only horse in the race.

But we're still the damned coolest...

The day I was saved by a sweetie.

Nine ways to do something ten times better…read this and you'll never go back to doing that…20 steps to something else…everything you need to know about nothing you need to know…

The lists go on and on.

We have become addicts of lists with numbers and letters (well, some of us).

We learn what we need to know from other folk who have learned what they need to know from other folk with lists.

If sentences don't have numbers or letters in front of them, we pass them by. Our eyes tell the list centres in our brains that they contain little of interest.

Move on. Nothing to see here.

These aren't the lists you're looking for.

They're just ordinary words. In ordinary sentences. In ordinary paragraphs.

They are list-free zones.

They're extraordinary-free zones.

Yes…lists chop information down into easily digestible bites.

Yes…lists are handy when you want to scan text for the stuff that might be important.

Yes…lists help you get your priorities in order.

Yes…lists save you time and effort.

And don't get me started on bullet points or asterisks.

All good things. All great things, really.

I admit it. I used to love them.

Used them in my copy as much as possible.

First it was whenever I thought they'd help the copy.

Then, as the craving took hold, it was whenever I could fit them in.

Which was ridiculously often.

Until I realised that my copy wasn't copy any more.

There was no flow. No eloquence. No conversation. No rhyme. No reason. No extraordinary copy.

There was only the list.

It wasn't a pretty sight.

Until the day I was saved by a sweetie.

You know that feeling when, as a kid, there's that one sweetie you just love? The one that shouts to you, or whispers sweetie somethings in your ear?

So you eat it to the exclusion of every other sweetie?

And you eat it over and over and over again?

Until you feel sick?

For me it was Caramac bars.

Buttery, melt-in-the-mouth caramel heaven.

They were, at one time, my reason for getting out of bed in the morning.

I realised I had a problem when I ran out of pocket money and went into severe Caramac withdrawal.

It was a Saturday.

It took me all my willpower to drag myself back from the edge of Caramac-induced madness.

Slowly, I became a creature of moderation.

I was 10.

Bit by bit, I learned to ration my Caramacs. First to one a day. Then one a week.

Then one a month.

Now, whenever I'm writing copy and I feel it might need a little "10 ways to do this", or "20 steps to improve that", or the odd 13 bullet points…I take out the ancient Caramac bar I have in my desk drawer.

It's inedible now, of course. Years past its sell-by date.

But it still speaks to me.

One look and it reminds me that moderation isn't just a collection of ten letters.

One word and it puts me right back on track.

Then I put it back in the drawer.

Until the next list…

The tiger, the goose, and picking on someone your own size.

I have a recurring nightmare.
I've had it, every few years, for as long as I can remember.
In it, I'm being chased by a tiger.
The beast eventually corners me on a milk float.
In desperation, I look around, see a fat goose standing minding its own business, grab it by the neck, swing it around my head, and wallop the tiger on the nose with the startled bird's rear end.
The giant cat roars as much with hurt pride as bruised nasal passages, and bounds away, tail between its legs, leaving me physically unharmed and emotionally unscarred.
The goose, fuelled by its newfound fighting prowess (by proxy), chases the tiger down the road, around a corner, and out of sight.
An almighty dust-up ensues and, after a few minutes, the goose reappears, a few feathers missing here and there, but smacking its wings together triumphantly like a pair of giant hands, having given the tiger a jolly good thrashing.
It looks at me, nods in satisfaction, and says, "Maybe next time the damned cat will pick on someone its own size." Then it takes to the air and glides off into a golden sky, like some nameless masked cowboy riding off into the sunset.
Sans Tonto the duck.
Now the only reason I mention this is that I was reminded yesterday how much I love to see the little guys of the world sticking it to the big guys.
Case in point...

Sometimes it's not the dog in the fight but the fight in the dog.

On Saturday 18th February, 2017, in the FA Cup, lowly (but tear-jerkingly gutsy) minnows Lincoln City became the first non-league team since QPR in 1914 to reach the Cup's last eight. And they did it by beating Premier League side Burnley Football Club. (31)

Eighty-one places above them.

Eighty bloody one.

The crowd went wild.

The latest tale of giant-killing magic was written large in FA Cup history.

Or…

Another case in point.

Lucky Generals was a London-based independent creative agency, launched by Helen Calcraft, Andy Nairn and Danny Brooke-Taylor in 2013

It was a small gun, often pitching for business in a world full of big guns.

But it knew how to damned well shoot.

Not long after it opened its doors, Lucky Generals created a modest, but perfectly formed, piece of CSR work for Paddy Power.

The work generated around 400 MILLION impressions, give or take, across social media in a single week, and eventually led to the agency winning the £25M creative account outright. (32)

It just goes to show.

It's not always about how big your guns are.

Sometimes it's all about how bloody good your aim is…

Always keep your pitchfork handy.

There was a time when snake oil salesmen didn't have to work very hard to be believed.

Their customers and potential customers were a trusting lot.

They didn't ask for, or expect, much in life.

Only that people were honest with them.

Didn't lie to them through their teeth.

Gave them the real dope. The straight stuff. The Gospel truth.

The snake oil salesmen relied on this. Played on it. Thrived on it.

Used it to advertise and sell their wares and make their money.

The words legal, honest, and decent were alien concepts to them.

The words charlatan, crook, and mountebanks should have been more appropriate.

However…

There was nobody around to look out for their customers. Nobody to protect them from the mountebanks.

Until pitchforks were invented.

And people realised that oil of vipers was as effective as a chocolate fireguard. Except to vipers.

It didn't mend their bones. Didn't cure rheumatism, neuralgia, sciatica, paralysis of the limbs, treat animal or insect bites. It did nothing for bunions, either. And sometimes did more harm than good.

But it did do one thing very successfully. It brought hope…then stomped all over it.

Then angry mobs, realizing they'd been duped, grabbed their pitchforks and ran snake oil salesmen out of town.

Under threat of verbal violence and multiple puncture wounds.

Customers and potential customers had learned a thing or three. Things like:

Never believe something just because somebody else says it's true

Always keep your pitchfork tines nicely sharpened.

But mostly, how to spot snake oil salesmen a mile away.

It worked for a while.

But snake oil salesmen were sneaky.

They adapted.

They became legitimate. Sort of.

They learned a thing or three, too. Things like:

Never make a claim without backing it up with dubious evidence. From people customers had never heard of.

Never offer a money back guarantee (especially if the customer is still alive).

And never, never, NEVER, produce anything without including the requisite amount of warnings about side effects. In very small print.

It worked for a while.

But customers were clever.

They became knowledgeable.

They learned what worked and what didn't work.

They learned about medicine and healthcare.

They learned about solid, scientifically proven evidence.

They learned about advertising that didn't lie through its teeth.

And they went back to being a trusting lot.

But they never, never, NEVER, forgot where they kept their pitchforks.

Because snake oil salesmen were still sneaky…

The grumpier you are, the longer you might live.

I have a theory about memory. It goes something like this.

The place in the brain where memory resides is split into two parts.

Part One is for good memories. All the people and events in your life that make you smile bring you happiness. Make you feel warm and fuzzy. Part Two is for bad memories. All the people and events in your life that make you sad and bring you pain. Make you feel and look like shit.

I have another theory about memory. It's linked to the first theory. It goes something like this.

Most people are born with both parts (One and Two) intact and fully working.

However, some people are born with Part One missing. And to compensate for this, they have an overactive Part Two.

They worry (constantly). They don't celebrate success.

They can only remember the bad things in life. Never the good.

They always look on the dark side of life. Never the bright side.

Cue whistle…

Give them some good news and they'll instantly look for the downside.

Give them some bad news and they'll never look for the upside.

Show them possibilities and they'll only see impossibilities.

Overactive Part Two people are pessimists. And their champion is Victor Meldrew.

He has us in stitches and yet he doesn't have a single funny bone in his body.

But what he does have is the ability to last a few years longer than most before he kicks the bucket.

According to Frieder R. Lang, lead author of a study by the University of Erlangen-Nuremberg in Germany, older people blighted by pessimism and fear for the future are more likely to live longer.

Whether they want to or not is another matter.

The study, into 40,000 adults across ten years, found those with low expectations for a "satisfying future" actually led healthier lives. (33)

In contrast, people who were "overly optimistic" about the future had a greater risk of disability or death.

Whether they like it or not.

Another study, The Deloitte Millennial Survey 2017 was based on a poll of more than 8,000 millennials across 30 countries. It found that young Aussies are more down on life than their global counterparts, particularly when it comes to economic stability.

Maybe they're planning to live longer down under. Buggered economy and World's highest melanoma shit not withstanding.

Personally, I don't give a tinker's cuss whether I live to 75 with a walking stick or 105 with a wheelchair.

Turns out I'm not one of life's Victor Meldrews after all.

My determination and ability to be optimistic about the future are, I feel, enough medicine to keep me as young as I want to feel. Between my ears, that is. Apart from all the legally prescribed mood-enhancing drugs available.

But that's another story.

My desire to see the funny side of life…to laugh when maybe I should be crying…to flip the bird to the seriously UNfunny, grumpy side of life…these are things that make the journey worth taking.

These are things that have my permission to put as many damned laughter lines on my face as they want.

This is why humour in advertising will always have a place in MY world.

Not always…but often enough.

This is why beautifully written and shown information that makes me smile will persuade me to buy something far quicker than a bunch of words and pictures giving me just the facts. Powerful though they may be.

That the sales pitch might be delivered by a straight faced, uber-grumpy Victor Meldrew or Basil Fawlty is an irony that isn't lost on me.

I'll laugh all the way to my wallet…

Big ideas, damp squibs, and a bridge too far.

Two words.
Six letters.
A million possibilities.
What if…
The kind of phrase that unbuckles the straitjackets, opens the windows, and lets the fresh air in.
The kind of phrase that ramps up the speed limit on the highway that leads from the parietal lobe up to the occipital lobe in our cerebral cortex. You know…that spongy bit of grey matter that sits between our ears.
The kind of phrase that sits at the heart of every work of fiction (and some would say fact) created by every writer who ever lived.
The kind of phrase that lets the imagination off the leash and gives it the freedom to go wherever the Hell it wants to.
For instance…
What if…you could take key elements of the plays of William Shakespeare and blend them into the most successful space movie franchises of all time?
What if… you could create a device that fits in your pocket and is MILLIONS of times smarter than all the computers used on the Apollo moon landing in the 60s?
What if…agencies stopped wasting billions making ads that were dull and uninspiring, and started investing billions telling stories that were fascinating, motivating, and empowering?

What if…NO creative director, writer, art director, visualizer, digital designer, senior, junior, tea or coffee making junior, could begin any piece of work without a comprehensive, well-written, briefing document. Printed out on paper and signed off.

Ever!

Hang on…that last one might be a bridge too far.

Ok. How about this, then…

The late, great, Bill Bernbach said, and I quote, "Advertising is fundamentally persuasion…and persuasion happens to be not a science, but an art."

Which means it's less about how many cans of beans you can sell…and more about how many cans of beans you can persuade folk to buy.

And here's another What If.

A big one.

What if…Creative Departments everywhere refused to produce any piece of work until they were absolutely, positively, unquestionably sure that it had a big idea somewhere inside it?

What? Another bridge too far?

Okay. Fine. Here's another 'late, great' quote instead.

This one's from David Ogilvy.

You might have heard of him.

It goes like this…

"It takes a big idea to attract the attention of consumers and get them to buy your product. Unless your advertising contains a big idea, it will pass like a ship in the night. I doubt if more than one campaign in a hundred contains a big idea."

One in a bloody hundred.

Just think about that for a minute.

Now think about this.

In March 2016, media research agency ZenithOptimedia reported that global advertising expenditure was on course to grow 4.6% to $579 BILLION that year. Up from 3.9% growth the previous year.

Imagine the whole of the fiscal defense budget for the USA for 2017. [34]

Or a space the size of a football field stacked over 6 ft. high with £100 dollar bills.

That's roughly what $579 billion would look like.

Give or take.

And not more than one campaign in 100 has a big idea.

That's not a lot of bang for our advertising bucks.

In fact it's more like a damp bloody squib.

Here's a thought.

What if…big ideas were compulsory?

Not merely optional.

What if they were at the core of every piece of creative work?

Not just at the core of the best of them.

Or is that just another damned bridge too far?

Ashes, self-injury, and peanut butter.

It's no big secret that today is Ash Wednesday.

It's also no big secret that, as the years go by and society changes, the term Ash Wednesday will probably mean less and less to more and more people.

I can remember as a youngster going to mass and coming away from the altar with a dark ashy thumbprint on my forehead. Courtesy of the local priest.

Around the world millions of churchgoers will probably end up washing their foreheads when they get home from mass.

However…I won't be one of them.

Nowadays my church is an internal thing…not an external one.

Instead, I will be marking these 24 hours for two very different reasons.

The first is that today is SIAD, or Self-injury Awareness Day.

It's painfully shocking to learn that each year, 1 in 5 females and 1 in 7 males engage in self-injury. [35]

So I will be thinking of all those who do (for whatever reason) and quietly sending them my very best wishes.

On a less painful note, my second reason for celebrating, is that today is National Peanut Butter Lover's Day.

I suspect it's observed mainly in the US.

But today I am extending the celebrations to here in the UK. And to a PB&J lover's home somewhere in the North West of England in particular.

Mine.

I will celebrate by munching my way through more than a few sandwiches liberally coated in the brown ambrosia.

Smooth, salted variety only.

You might see a few more advertisements in the press or on the telly for peanut butter. Smooth and crunchy varieties.

I wish there were one or two for Self-injury Awareness Day.

Or three…or four…

We've come a long way since Gilgamesh.

I've been a writer for most of my life.

But, more importantly, I've been a reader for longer.

Books have always been my preferred mode of transport.

With them, I've travelled fantastic journeys across the inner landscape of my imagination.

Like everyone, I have my favourites.

In between their covers, I've lived a thousand lives vicariously. Listened to a million voices tell their stories.

With them, I've never felt alone. They've always been generous with their companionship.

I could read books every waking hour of every day, and still not even begin to scratch the surface of everything available to me.

But this day is special.

This day, March 2, is World Book Day, 2017.

Officially we've only had a World Book Day once a year for the past 20 years.

Unofficially, World Book Day has existed for as long as there have been people around to write books. And people around to read them.

Whatever their age.

The Epic of Gilgamesh is the oldest-known written story that can claim any right to be called a book. It was written in ancient Sumeria sometime prior to the 18th century B.C. on clay tablets.

We've come a long way since that progenitor.

According to Google's advanced algorithms, around 130 million books have been published between then and now.

Doesn't sound much, really.

But that's merely the number of unique titles.

That doesn't even begin to cover the number of actual books printed.

Some numbers are just too big to take on board without a large whisky.

So today, on World Book Day, I plan to do something to celebrate all that print…on all that paper…from all those minds.

It won't be big. But it will be something I've never done before.

I'm going to pick up a book. Any book. It really doesn't matter which one.

I'll open it up.

I'll read the first sentence of the first paragraph on the first page.

Then the next sentence. And the next one.

Hell, I might even read the whole damned page.

Aloud.

Wherever I am.

But the voice I hear won't be mine.

It will be the voice of Gilgamesh.

Calling to me from the past.

Reminding me where it all started…

There are suits...and then there are SUITS!!

I remember the first suit I came across, in the first ad agency I joined.

He was a gnat's whisker over 20 years old and constantly loud.

It was a coping mechanism for lack of confidence.

He wore a cheap off-the-peg grey number, a red tie permanently undone, and brogues with a shine that was duller than dishwater.

Or ditchwater.

His teeth were crooked and stained.

The middle and index fingers of his right hand were yellow with nicotine. His breath smelled like a well-used ashtray. And he thought he was the dog's bollocks.

He wasn't, of course.

He was the dogsbody.

The gofer on the bottom rung of the ladder

But because he also possessed the gift of the gab, he was tolerated.

And because he was as keen as mustard, he was encouraged.

He had arrived from college (with a detour at his uncle's estate agency) and pretty quickly discovered what it felt like to be thrown in at the deep end...sans water wings.

That was 30-odd years ago and at the time there were a lot like him.

Then something changed. He learned how to swim.

And gradually he turned from a suit into a SUIT!!

He knuckled down.

Came up the hard way.
Learned his trade.
Developed a serious face.
Stopped smoking.
Learned how to dress properly.
Moved agencies a few times.
Sorted out his teeth.
And turned into a damned good Account Director.
Clients loved him.
Suits under him loved him.
Creative Directors loved him.

He didn't just present campaigns to clients, he sold them like his life depended on it.

Of course sometimes the best ideas he presented sold themselves. He simply sat back and refused to take the credit.

Which is why writers and art directors loved him, too.

No new marketing development escaped his attention. As time went on and the future beckoned, he embraced the digital creative revolution and all things social media with the fervor and passion of a true believer.

He was old school and new school. He was past, present, and future.

All his rough edges had been buffed smooth as silk.
He had gravitas.
And style.
And experience.
And a damned fine tailor.

Eventually, he became a respected board director, with special responsibility for the acquisition and training of talent.

Who better, his fellow directors reasoned, to oversee the pursuit and mentoring of raw newbies, than someone who had clawed his way up from the dark pit and into the bright light.

Someone who truly, madly, deeply understood the difference between a suit...and a SUIT!!

Everything changes, but nothing is truly lost.

When I was young and before a Gillette blade ever touched my face, I used to attend a good old-fashioned boys-only grammar school.

In Battersea, London.

Not too far from the power station.

Before it was decommissioned and redeveloped.

James Bond was an old boy there.

At the school, not the power station.

At the time he was simply known as young Roger Moore.

Or so his MI6 cover story went.

The curriculum included four live languages. English, French, Spanish, and German.

And one (almost) dead one.

Latin.

At the time, I could never understand why a language that hadn't been spoken by the great unwashed for about 1,500 years, was still hanging on for a last gasp at life in classrooms in the 20th century. As it was then.

I never took to it. And as far as I know it never took to me either.

However, I didn't realise how sneaky it was.

Latin wasn't dead. It was just resting.

Waiting for me.

Fast forward thirty or so years, and I chose two short Latin words as the title for one of my books. Or maybe they chose me.

Ad Lib.

The book is an off-the-cuff, improvised collection of personal thoughts and observations based on my life as a copywriter.

And life in general.

The name seems to fit like a second skin. The first one being already in place.

I chose another two Latin words for the title of this short tale, taken from the book.

Carpe Diem.

Seize the day.

I seized the day when I changed tracks and went from my first job working in Soho to my next job working in Fleet Street.

I seized it when I went from working in newspapers to working in advertising.

I seized it when I went from being an agency copywriter to being a freelancer.

And I seized it when I decided to add another string to my bow.

That of being an author.

I am, I fear, a habitual seizer.

To this end, I have another Latin phrase waiting in the wings.

This one's a four-worder.

I bring it out and say it aloud, it every time I carpe the hell out of any passing diem.

It's from a book titled The Sandman, Vol.10. The Wake.

By author Neil Gaiman.

It goes like this.

Omnia Mutantur, Nihil Interit.

Or, as we who have some fleeting familiarity with resting languages would say:

Everything changes, but nothing is truly lost.

Amen to that…

Mistakes, copy-checkers, and Billy Faulkner.

On November 13, 1789, Benjamin Franklin (Benny to his mates), picked up his finest quill, dipped it in his best ink, and wrote a letter to the French scientist, Jean-Baptiste Leroy.

In it, he said, "…nothing can be said to be certain except death and taxes."

As far as we know, he was the first person to bring that thought to life and put it down on paper.

Now, over 200 years later, I'd like to add a third certainty to that painfully short list.

Human error.

We are a not a perfect species.

Never have been.

Hopefully never will be.

We can get some of the things right all of the time.

We can get all of the things right some of the time.

But we'll never, EVER, get all of the things right all of the time.

Sooner or later we always screw up.

Sooner or later we always fall down.

We do the wrong things for the right reasons…and the right things for the wrong reasons…with alarming regularity.

Making mistakes, it seems, is in our DNA.

Even the very words we speak and write are riddled with opportunities to bugger things up.

Many years ago, an ad agency where I worked employed a copy checker.

She didn't just check that all the right words had all the right letters…in all the right places.

She road tested for things like logic flaws, mixed metaphors, non sequiturs, typographical errors, grammatical faults, contractions, contradictions, wrong tenses, misplaced apostrophes, and a hundred other possible blunders.

She also sense-checked the hell out of it.

She knew that, even although any writer worth their salt should take full responsibility for the accuracy of their own copy, they occasionally get lazy. Slip up. Drop the ball. Screw the pooch.

She didn't.

She was worth her weight in gold.

To the agency and to the agency's clients.

She lived to find the errors that we ordinary creative mortals let slip through our careless brains and fingers.

As a young(ish) copywriter I lived to thwart her efforts.

My thwarting, however, was a hit and miss affair.

More often than not, she found something that made me rethink, rewrite, or just plain kick myself. Sometimes all three.

I didn't always agree with her.

But she kept me on my toes.

And made me a better writer.

And a better speller.

There's one thing that Ernest Hemingway, William Faulkner, F. Scott Fitzgerald, John Keats, and Jane Austin all had in common.

Apart from the obvious.

They might have been great writers…but they were without exception pretty crap spellers.

In Faulkner's case, whenever his newspaper editors complained about his spelling, he'd retort, "Well, that's what you're hired to correct."

Literary giant that he was, Billy could also be a real jerk.

Every now and then, I come across copy that was obviously written by someone who belongs in Faulkner's camp. Well…as far as the spelling is concerned anyway.

And when I do, I wish that every creative department in every agency had a damned good copy checker.
Just to keep the writers on their toes.
Just to make them better…

I used to write by the light of the silvery moon.

Years ago I used to write my best copy when most of the rest of the world, in my time zone anyway, had gone to sleep.
Even then there was always lots of room for improvement.
Still is.
Always will be.
Didn't matter who the client was.
Or what the product or service was.
Didn't matter whether the copy was short or long.
Whether it was for print, radio, online, or tv.
I'd draft during the day and rewrite during the night.
When the moon came out my juices started to flow.
It was almost a primal feeling.
The darkness acted like a catalyst, enhancing the lunar ebb and flow of my fingers across the keyboard.
The 2am lack of distraction was a drug and I was a silence junkie.
Insomnia was a constant companion.
That was back in the day when I could write all night and the only fuel I needed was a constant supply of strong, black coffee.
And a few milk chocolate biscuits.
But times change.
Internal clocks have a habit of going AWOL.
Off on their own journeys.
And before I knew it, writing by the light of the silvery moon was a first class pain in the ass.

I got real weary before I got real good.

So I switched to writing early in the morning.

Real early.

I'd punch my card, clock on for the 5am shift, set up the De'Longhi, and lay down some words as the first rays of dawn danced across the rooftops.

My ideal breakfast was a great headline.

And great coffee.

My ideal morning was great body copy.

And more coffee.

Trouble was, my afternoons and evenings were shot to Hell.

So now I've switched to writing when the sun comes up.

And stays up.

Up, where everyone else on my side of the world, on my side of the creative fence, does what they do best. With both eyes open and a full frontal lobe that isn't half asleep.

Up, where there's noise, and music, and voices, and life. And where stories are fashioned from more than just words on a page, or pixels on a screen.

Up, where my circadian rhythm is back where it belongs. Where my pulse has the soft percussive feel of a cool conga drum. And where my synapses can dance the Hairy Mambo all the way from Aberdeen to Zanzibar and back again.

Without breaking sweat...

How I discovered the sound of my third voice.

Let me tell you a story.
I come from a family of enthusiastic talkers.
When I was young, I was told on more than one occasion that I liked the sound of my own voice.
It wasn't meant as a compliment.
Or an insult.
It was merely an observation, made by those on the receiving end, on how damned overactive my voice box was.
Especially when it came to giving my opinion free rein.
Which I did with vigorous abandon.
I was still in single digits.
I was a talker.
Still am, truth be told.
My constant chatter was a natural phenomenon.
After a while, I became much more interested in the meaning of the sounds, rather than just the sounds themselves.
So I became a reader.
Then, after another while, I became much more interested in creating my own combination of words. My own stories.
So I became a writer.
And I discovered that my words had a voice that had nothing to do with the sounds they made when spoken aloud.
Nothing to do with the physical characteristics of my larynx.
And everything to do with the physical characteristics of my readers' ears.

Whenever I spoke, the voice I heard was transmitted via my jawbone into my brain.

What everyone else heard was a voice transmitted via the air and into their ear canal.

They weren't the same.

That's why recorded me sounded different to natural me. With recorded me I heard what everyone else heard. It was nearly the same as natural me.

But not quite.

I had two voices.

And one source.

Then, slowly, I began to hear a third voice.

One that had nothing to do with soundwaves.

And everything to do with personality.

Identity.

Presence.

Letters.

I could hear this third voice in everything I wrote.

I still can.

And every time I pick up a pen or place the tips of my fingers onto my keyboard, it feel like I'm opening a door and greeting an old friend.

I always will.

I have three voices.

And one source…

Trombones, swooning, and hanging on every word.

Early on in his career, the late, great, Francis Albert Sinatra realised how important a very special breathing technique was to the way he sang.

And to the way people reacted to his voice.

The technique was called circular breathing, and he learned it by watching big band leader Tommy Dorsey play the trombone.

Using it, he developed a style of singing that allowed him to stretch a musical phrase far longer than normal.

He took fewer pauses for breath.

He learned to do more with the air he had.

As a result, young, impressionable teenage girls…and just as many slightly older impressionable ladies… hung on to every note Frankie boy sang.

And they kept on hanging on.

And on…

Then some of them promptly fell over.

Chests heaving.

Gasping for breath.

They hadn't learned the art of circular breathing.

But they had perfected something else.

The art of swooning with sheer emotion.

Or, as they call it in the medical profession, lack of oxygen.

Years later, many of the fans of Elvis, The Beatles and The Rolling Stones (and many others) suffered the same fate.

They hung on to every word The King, John, Paul, and Mick sang. Screamed their heads off. Then promptly keeled over.

Clever writers know this phenomenon.

They know that getting their readers to hang on to every sentence they write is like reaching out and touching the Holy Grail.

But they know it has nothing to do with religion.

Or music.

And everything to do with rhythm.

Not the kind that moves bodies. But the kind that moves words. And, more importantly, readers.

Put simply…good rhythm in a sentence makes it eminently more readable.

Bad rhythm in a sentence sucks.

Big time.

The words you use. The way they scan. The pauses in between the phrases. The breaks in between the sentences. The length of the sentences. The way your readers say them in their heads.

Get it spot on and you could have them hanging on your every word.

They'll probably read whatever you write.

They might even become big fans.

But as for swooning, don't hold your breath…

The best ideas come as jokes.

I have a nightmare.

It comes calling every now and then. Just to throw rocks at me.

It's very specific.

And it goes something like this…

I'm in a room with a damned good art director and four suits (three account handlers and somebody sitting quietly taking notes).

The suits have come mob-handed.

There's a table and six chairs. The room doesn't have any windows. It doesn't have a door.

We can't escape.

I need to go to the loo.

On the table in front of each of us is a Creative Brief. It's typed on one side of a single sheet of paper. In a foreign language.

The account handlers talk through the brief. I can't understand them.

Neither can the art director.

When they finish they smile, then along with the note taker they disappear into thin air, leaving just me and the art director in the room.

All alone.

With no means of escape. No means of knowing what the brief is about. No means of knowing what we're supposed to do. And no means of knowing how long we've got, to do whatever we're supposed to do.

Then we notice the giant egg timer.

It's made of glass, full of sand, and the sand is starting to flow from the top compartment to the bottom one. There's a sign carved into the wooden frame that supports the timer.

The sign says: "Coming up with a great idea takes time. You have two hours."

This is usually when I wake up covered in sweat.

My heart pounding in my chest.

This is usually when I have to remind myself that I have absolutely no idea where great ideas come from.

This is usually when I realise I am about to lose all bladder control.

I have always been of the opinion that great ideas don't give a damn where they come from. They don't give a damn who has them or where or when.

All they know is that they're great ideas.

I know creatives who set out on the hunt for a great idea first thing in the morning. With lots of coffee and plenty of cerebral interplay.

I know creatives who head for the nearest bar as soon as possible after opening time, and rely on strong liquid refreshment to kickstart the whole process.

I know creatives who have their best ideas while they're sitting on the loo…or standing in the shower…or lying in bed, just before they drift off to sleep.

I know creatives who sit, silently staring at the wall, until something happens between their ears that brings a lightbulb moment to life.

And I know creatives who seem to be blessed with an open invitation to visit the cosmic library of great ideas whenever they feel like it…and stay as long as they like.

Bastards…

Sadly, I also know creatives who think they simply don't have the time to have a great idea. They're too busy getting anything down on paper before their allotted time runs out.

They're too busy putting the cart before the horse.

They're too busy trying to produce quantity. Not quality.

David Ogilvy, one of the few genuine legends in advertising, and co-founder of Ogilvy & Mather, famously said: "The best ideas come as jokes. Make your thinking as funny as possible."

I have another nightmare.

It comes calling every now and then. Just to throw beer bottles at me.

It's very specific.

And it goes something like this…

I'm on stage at a comedy club. I'm holding the mic stand to stop myself from shaking.

The mic stand is shaking.

I'm looking out into the darkness.

I know there are hundreds of people in the audience. I know they're getting ready to pee themselves laughing. I know they've come to see me be funny.

And for the life of me, I can't think of a damned thing to say…

Viv Stanshall, George Orwell, and Apples.

The year was 1970.

I was 19.

I remember being in a friend's house listening to music.

We were playing vinyl on his dad's Ferguson record player.

He slid his prized 'debut album' copy of Gorilla, by The Bonzo Dog Doo-Dah Band, onto the turntable. I was introduced to the unique talent that was Vivian Stanshall.

My friend carefully placed the stylus in the groove. Opened the window.

And we sat back and smoked something very slightly illicit.

Three tracks into side two, Big Shot came on.

I heard the following:

"Have you got a light mac?"

"No, but I've got a dark brown overcoat."

I nearly choked on my cider.

I've always loved that album. Especially those two lines.

Anyway…before I knew it, the year was 1985.

I was 34. A copywriter.

And I was watching a video of 1984.

Not the movie with Richard Burton and John Hurt.

The ground shattering television commercial that introduced the Apple Macintosh personal computer to the world.

The one where a blonde female athlete, carrying a large, brass-headed sledgehammer, runs towards an Orwellian "Big Brother" image on a huge screen.

The one conceived by Steve Hayden, Brent Thomas, and Lee Clow of Chiat/Day.

The one that Advertising Age placed on top of its list of the 50 greatest television commercials ever made.

The one that, for some unfathomable reason, was only ever aired twice on American television.

Some called it a dystopian masterpiece. Others called it the best damned commercial ever directed by Ridley Scott.

I was too busy picking my jaw up off the floor to call it anything.

It switched on parts of me that I didn't even realise were switched off. And it made me go out and buy my first Apple computer.

I've been buying them ever since.

That original one was a light coloured Mac 128K. I bought it during the summer of 1985.

The next one was definitely a bit of a classic. Just like Gorilla. I bought it during the really cold winter of 1990.

By then, I already had my dark brown overcoat…

You can't use up creativity.

In an interview in 1982, the late (and great) American poet, memoirist and civil rights activist Maya Angelou said the following:

"You can't use up creativity. The more you use, the more you have."

Fifty-two letters. Thirteen words. Two sentences.

I think those sentences should be printed in a cool typeface, on quality card, and handed to every person (young or not so) who joins every creative department of every advertising agency.

I think they should be on the front cover of their agency welcome pack brochure.

If they get one.

I think those 13 words should be printed in bold by agencies on the birthday cards to their staff, every year, just to remind them that chronology has bugger all to do with creativity. And everything to do with simply growing older.

Some more gracefully than others.

I love the vitality, enthusiasm, barefaced audacity, fun, energy, spunk, insubordination, and just-damned-well-do-it-and-bugger-the-consequences bravery of young creatives.

I love their hunger. Their removal of the safety net.

They have no idea how much they don't know. And sometimes they couldn't give a damn.

Sometimes they just want to rip it up and start again.

I love it...even though I don't always agree with it. Even though it annoys the hell out of me sometimes.

But that's only because my head doesn't live in their part of the forest any more.

It's still the same forest.

Just a different clearing.

I'm older. Not necessarily always wiser. More experienced. Not necessarily always more knowledgeable.

Just as creative. Just not always as wrinkle-free.

There's a quote, attributed to Pablo Picasso, which, for me, sums it up very nicely. Almost.

"Youth has no age."

It just needs another line tagged onto the end. Just to finish it off.

"Same goes for creativity."

Thirty-four letters. Eight words. Two sentences.

Truth damn well told...

Numbers and Letters.

I've never been a big fan of numbers.

The thought of sitting down and losing myself in mathematics has been known to bring me out in a nasty rash. I develop itches in hard to reach places.

It's not that I'm incapable of computation. Give me a poke in the guts with a sharp stick and I can be as numerate as the next guy. Almost.

I just have no overpowering interest in figuring out figures. And, as far as I can tell, they have no overpowering interest in figuring out me.

Letters, however, are a completely different story.

Letters make my skin tingle, my juices flow, and my tongue slowly stroke the inside edges of my lips.

Computers communicate with numbers. Nature communicates with numbers.

Humans (well, most of us anyway) communicate with touch, sound, and letters.

With them, I can make sense of the world around me. Or try to. With them, I can make sense of the world inside me. Or try to.

The phrase; "I write, therefore I am," was twisted not long after I came into the world. It now reads; "I am, therefore I write."

Ad Lib is one of the latest products of that writing.

I wrote it after I had spent a few decades in the advertising business. More accurately in the creative part of the advertising business.

But this isn't a 'how to' book. I have no wish (or right) to tell anyone how to do anything. Too many folk are doing that already.

This is more like a 'what' book. Occasionally a "why" book. With lots of casual observations and opinions on advertising in particular and the human condition in general.

It won't change your life.

It won't forgive your sins.

It won't improve your health.

It's not serious enough to take on those kind of responsibilities.

But hopefully it will help you slow down and pass a few enjoyable and peaceful hours reading...while the rest of the world goes about its business, giving itself ulcers with powerful enthusiasm.

Enjoy...

Bowstrings, Plugs, and Dirty Harry Callahan.

The year was 1973.

I was 22.

I was in The Odeon cinema Leicester Square, London. Watching the movie Magnum Force, starring Clint Eastwood as kick-ass cop Dirty Harry Callahan.

The sequel to his more iconic movie Dirty Harry.

He still had his .44 Magnum. The most powerful handgun in the world. Well, it was then.

The famous quote from his previous outing in the movie Dirty Harry was still at the back of my mind.

"You've got to ask yourself one question. Do I feel lucky? Well, do ya, punk?"

But it was the last line of this new movie that would stick in my mind for much longer.

"A man's got to know his limitations."

I thought Harry got that one wrong. Dead wrong. Damned wrong.

I thought it was all kinds of wrong way back then...and I still think so now.

If I knew my limitations, I wouldn't have changed from working in the Daily Mirror to becoming an advertising copywriter.

New bowstring.

If I knew my limitations, I wouldn't have changed from being uncomfortably single to being happily married with children.

Another bowstring.

If I knew my limitations, I wouldn't have changed from being a staffing copywriter to being a freelancer.

Another bowstring.

And if I knew my limitations, I wouldn't have changed from being a copywriter to being a copywriter AND an author.

Latest bowstring.

Now for the plug.

The year is 2017.

My first book Love & Coffee, came out on Amazon last year. My latest one, Heaven Help Us, came out on Amazon last week.

It's about a sentient asteroid that threatens to crash into Earth, wiping out all life.

It's a bit of a comedy.

I've often wondered where I would be, and what I would be doing, if I'd taken Harry's advice, and acknowledged my limitations.

What might have happened if I'd stayed inside the box instead of stepping outside it.

The other day a friend and ex-colleague told me that he was finally getting around to writing the book he'd been meaning to write for years.

I almost punched the air in delight.

Maybe inside us all is the desire to add another string to our bow.

Maybe somewhere inside Harry, a little voice, straight out of Sudden Impact, would drawl:

"Go ahead, make my day!"

Snake oil, rocks, and watershed moments.

I've always had a soft spot for snakes.
Not so much for snake oil salesmen.
Had I been around in their heyday, I would probably have thrown rocks at them. The men, that is.
I would probably have hissed at them.
Or subjected them to a dose of venomous criticism.
Call it revenge by proxy.
Although those pioneering medical marketeers (and I use the term loosely) fascinated me a little, the shit they got away with pissed me off a whole lot more.
I tried to admire their enthusiasm and one-cure-fits-all sales techniques.
I failed miserably.
I tried to excuse their quackery and shortage of moral principles.
I crashed and burned.
I tried to see any plus side to their lack of accountability. And their callous disregard for the wellbeing of their customers.
All I saw was my theoretical pile of handy throwing rocks growing larger by the minute.
The problem was this...
In a world where good health was in short supply and marketing regulations were non-existent, the guys with the miracle elixirs and dubious ethical codes could concoct whatever they wanted.
Claim whatever they wanted.
And charge whatever they wanted.

And few people had the guts, good health, medical knowledge, legal recourse, or legal firearms, to argue the toss.

Because the guys with the foul-tasting liquid pedalled the one thing that everybody desperately needed.

Hope.

And hope came with fancy names.

In serious looking bottles.

With a long list of false promises.

By the time folk realised the truth, the snake oil salesmen were in the next town. Or the next county. Or, occasionally, the next life.

There was no accountability and no quick cure. For anything. Only a sinking feeling of being well and truly conned right up the wazoo.

Times were tough, elixirs were crap, and professional, responsible healthcare was a million miles away. But it was getting closer.

Fast forward to a sizeable watershed moment in 1955.

Commercial TV began broadcasting and, for the first time ever, ads were controlled by formal legislation.

Then in 1961, the Advertising Association joined together with other likeminded associations and grew teeth.

And they promptly legislated the hell out of anything anyone could claim in print, newspapers, posters, direct mail, and billboards, too.

And so was born the British Code of Advertising Practice.

Another fast forward. This time into the 21st century.

Over 50 years on, and advertising in the UK overwhelmingly sticks to the rules. Compliance surveys regularly reveal that more than 97% of ads are in line with the Advertising Codes. But sadly not 100%. [36]

There are still a few snake oil salesmen left.

They've improved their elixirs.

They've improved their sales techniques.

And they're bloody good at dodging rocks...

All the right letters. Just not necessarily in the right order.

I remember eating Alphabetti Spaghetti as a kid.

It was introduced by Heinz about 1930, (well before my time) and I always thought it was a brilliant way to help kids learn how to spell, have fun, and have food, all at the same time.

Discontinued in 1990, it was brought back like a prodigal snack, in 2005. [37] The A to Z of fun returned to children's meals.

Whether their spelling improved is another matter.

I never quite took to Alphabet Soup. Too much liquid. Not enough gooey playability.

For me, Alphabetti Spaghetti was the bee's knees of the single-digit kid's snack world.

In fact I put my spelling prowess, developed during my formative years, down to a deep-seated desire to put all the right letters absolutely in the right order.

It helped me discover the world of words. They were fun. They were easy. I couldn't understand how they could be so painfully difficult for anyone else.

Then one day I discovered the world of dyslexia.

A friend of mine was a sufferer. The condition haunted him all his life.

He used to say "pasghetti" a lot. His parents were Italian. They ate lots of pasta. He refused to eat the tinned alphabetti variety. He said he hated the taste.

He admitted the truth years later. He hated being reminded that, no matter how hard he tried putting the right letters in the right order before he put them into his mouth, they still sounded all wrong when they came back out of it.

According to the British Dyslexia Association, 10% of the population are dyslexic. Around 4% severely so. Around 40 million Americans are dyslexic...and only 2 million know they are.

Pause for thought.

I'm a writer. Have been most of my life. Awake and asleep.

I don't have dyslexia. I have something else instead. (Long story).

I'll probably be a writer until they screw the coffin lid on.

I can't imagine doing anything else. It's as natural to me now as breathing.

So when I discovered that 1 in 10 people are dyslexic, I had a bit of a jaw drop moment. And it made me wonder.

How many of them rely on words to make a living? How many of them have a problem with saying or writing some of those words? How many are authors? Or actors?

Just for the record (and for my friend) here are a few names you might recognise. [38]

Agatha Christie. Best selling author of all time. Believed to have had a spelling disability called dysgraphia.

F. Scott Fitzgerald. One of the greatest American writers of the 20th century. Believed to have had a learning disability which was most likely dyslexia.

Dav Pilkey. Author and illustrator of the highly successful Captain Underpants series of children's books. Diagnosed with dyslexia at an early age.

Add to that Tom Cruise, Whoopi Goldberg, Orlando Bloom, Keira Knightley, Steven Spielberg...the list goes on...and on...and on. Oh, and while you're at it, toss in Albert Einstein. [39]

So I don't get annoyed when I see a misspelled word. Or hear the odd mispronounced one. Or more. It might be laziness or carelessness on the part of the writer or the speaker. Or it might be a condition such as dyslexia. One that can't be cured but CAN be managed. And acknowledged. And understood.

Final pause for thought.

On Thursday October 5th, 2017, it will be World Dyslexia Awareness Day.

It's smack dab in the middle of World Dyslexia Awareness Week. Also known as Monday October 2nd through to Sunday the 8th.

A week made up of all the right days. Arranged in exactly the right order...

(PS: My everlasting thanks to Eric Morecambe, Ernie Wise, Sid Green, Dick Hills, and André Previn. The best humour never grows old).

Advertising, DNA, and the echo of a scream.

I have this dream about the future of advertising.

In it, brilliant new marketing techniques will join with advanced DNA targeting and sophisticated social profiling.

The business will become so damned good at its job that consumers will receive only the ads that they want to see or hear. For the products and services that they definitely want or need. Offered by the manufacturers or suppliers that they're most likely to buy from.

Nothing more. Nothing less.

They won't even realise they're missing out on all the crap they don't want to know about.

In fact they won't even realise how much they don't realise.

They won't have to sift through the thousands (maybe millions) of sales messages they used to be subjected to. Every day. Every week. Every year.

They won't have to compare one product or service to another. Figure out which one rocks their boat more.

They won't have to listen to a mountain of sales pitches. Each one fighting for their attention. Every one fighting for their money.

They won't have to take the time, to expend the effort, to make the right decisions about price...product benefits...and a hundred other factors.

Factors that used to inform them. Persuade them. Help them decide what to buy, from whom, where, when, and for how much.

All that will be taken care of. Automatically.

All that will be paid for, too. Automatically. As long as sufficient funds are available for efficient removal from their bank account.

Personal preference will happen below the surface. At the cellular level.

Personal shopping will be a distant memory.

As will personal beliefs.

Pretty soon folk will be wearing the same clothes. Eating the same food. Drinking the same drink. Watching the same television programmes. Driving the same cars. Living the same lives. Saying the same words. Having the same thoughts.

All without batting an eyelid.

All without missing a beat.

That's usually when I wake up.

The echo of a scream in my head.

Breathless. Pulse racing. Bedclothes drenched in sweat. Only to realise, yet again, that it was just the tail end of another bad dream.

Only to realise that algorithms didn't really murder Mad Men and Women after all. It just seemed like they did, at first. The blood was fake.

Big data and always-on creativity look more and more like joined-at-the-hip lovers every day.

God bless their sweaty output.

I crawl out of bed and grab a strong coffee.

Then, just when I think everything's okay, just when I think everything's forward thinking and hunky dory...I realise I'm in a new dream. It's also an old one.

This one's about advertising in the past.

It features an ancient Creative Director I knew. He's looking at me with grim determination in his eyes. He's yelling at me with rage in his voice. He's hanging onto my wrists with tightly clenched fists.

And the brilliant bastard refuses to let go.

Punching B. Earl Puckett in the kisser.

I always thought that the business of advertising was just about making the customer happy.

Happy because they could learn how to afford at least some of the things they never thought they would be able to.

Happy because they could discover how to feel better, look better, and live better.

Happy because they could throw out the old things that didn't work properly and get new things that worked better than the old ones ever did.

Partners excluded, mostly.

Happy because they could learn more about the world, and the world could learn more about them.

Happy because they could see at least some of their dreams and aspirations come true.

Happy because they could be informed, impressed, entertained, enthralled, excited, inspired, motivated, and a whole lot of other 'eds". All just by looking at words and images on a page, or on a screen.

Or so I thought.

Then I came across B. Earl Puckett.

He was born in Wayne County, Michigan, USA, in 1879. Died, aged 78, in Fairfield Illinois. And he was the retired chairman of the Allied Stores Corporation. One of America's largest department store chains.

He was a genius with a knack for making something very good out of something very average.

He joined Allied in 1933, and by 1947 he had increased the company's annual profit from $25,000 to a whopping $20 million. [40]

His merchandising ideas are still apparent in today's modern megastores.

One day, someone asked this sales genius what he did for a living. This is what he said:

"It is our job to make women unhappy with what they have."

The first time I read it I felt like punching him in the kisser, for making women sad, and excluding men and children.

I was way too late. He died in 1957.

The second time I read it I heard a penny drop.

When B. Earl Puckett wanted to make people feel happy about parting with their hard-earned cash...he did two things.

He reminded them why they had every right to feel unhappy.

Then he followed that up by giving them a damned good reason to smile, be happy, and get their wallets or cheque books out.

Simple.

Powerful.

Effective.

Advertising and Puckett were always heading for the same destination.

Sometimes they just took different routes to get there.

Pretty often they were on the same damned train…

Leather jackets, eyepatches, and storytelling.

1951 was the year I came into the world.

In addition, it was the year that the term Fast Food was born.

Somewhere inside I have always felt a mysterious kinship with cheeseburgers.

Now I know why.

It was also the year that a new style of advertising was born. Courtesy of David Ogilvy, some 50 cent black eyepatches, and a small shirt-maker from Maine, called CF Hathaway.

Somewhere inside I have always felt a mysterious kinship with eyepatches.

Now I know why.

Hathaway, who had never spent a dime on advertising before, was planning to spend $30,000 to compete with bigger and better-known brands. (41)

Ogilvy handed over the eyepatches (bought on a whim) to his photographer and said: "Just shoot a couple of these to humour me. Then I'll go away and you can do the serious job."

When he saw the test shots with the eyepatch, he knew they'd created something special.

Without the patch, they had a campaign that sold shirts.

With it, they had something bigger. Something much more interesting.

They had a story.

Who was the man? What happened to him? Did he damage his eye? Did he lose it?

Within a week after the campaign began, every Hathaway shirt in New York was sold.

And the rest, as they say, is history.

I have never been a big fan of ads that merely tell me about the product.

I know what a shirt is.

I have always been a big fan of ads that tell stories about products.

George Lucas, iconic director, screenwriter, producer, and creator of the Star Wars and Indiana Jones movies (and founder of Industrial Light & Magic), said: "A special effect without a story is a pretty boring thing." And he should know.

Here's my twist on it.

An ad full of facts without a story attached is a pretty damned boring thing. And that's the truth.

A couple of weeks ago, I read something written by a guy called Scott Donaton. He said: "The best and most celebrated ads have always been those that tell great stories because the best creatives know the key to winning over consumers is to share stories that are worthy of their time."

Donaton is the Chief Content Officer at Digitas. Part of the Publicis Group. A global advertising and public relations outfit, and one of the world's "Big Four" agencies.

So he should know.

He wrote it in an article published in Adweek in April 2016.

The title of the article?

"Why brands need to skip the ads and start telling stories."

I couldn't agree more. I love telling stories. Especially if they have a mysterious kinship with me.

Like this one.

I bought a leather biker jacket a few years back from a second hand stall. It was old but in good nick. I asked the stallholder how much she wanted for it.

She said: "Give me a tenner."

I think she was looking after the stall for a friend.

I handed over the money, put on the jacket, walked away from the stall, and casually put my hand in one of the pockets. There was crumpled, world-weary tenner in it.

An old leather jacket is just an old leather jacket.

But a mysterious, crumpled, world-weary tenner in the pocket?

Now that's a story...

Beautiful letters make beautiful words.

There was a time when I believed that words were just made up of letters. That all I needed to do to appreciate all their various permutations, was put them together in the right order.
That was before I knew better.
That was before I had my eyes opened.
That was before I was introduced to the world of typography.
I was, and still am, an outsider looking in. Not the other way around.
To me, typography has always seemed more like a beautifully arcane magic art, rather than a skill of alphabetic design.
It's probably a bit of both.
The typographers I've known have all exhibited the same wonderful talent.
The ability to bring dead letters to life.
Where writers work their magic with meaning, typographers work theirs with curves, angles, and straight lines. And together they give language a beauty that's greater than the sum of all its individual parts.
I've always been a Helvetica man (although I do format my books in Times New Roman).
To the purist, it's a sans serif Grotesque typeface, inspired by and based on Akzidenz-Grotesk typeface created by Berthold around 1898.
Try saying that when you're three sheets to the wind. Or even four.

To fans (me included) Helvetica is a typeface that's simple...easy to read...lovely to look at...and extremely popular.

It was designed in Switzerland in 1957 by Max Miedinger and Eduard Hoffmann at the Haas type foundry. It was originally called Die Neue Haas Grotesk.

In 1960 they changed the name, thank God.

Since then, it has become the ubiquitous 'one font fits all' typeface. The 'go to' typeface with such a neutral personality that it has become one of the most popular in the world.

So...why do so many people hate it?

Why is it known in some circles as HELLvetica?

Simple.

It's everywhere.

And familiarity breeds contempt.

So why do I like it so much?

Am I a coward? Am I unadventurous? Am I boring? Do I lack imagination?

Well...no. No. No. And definitely no.

The truth of the matter is there's just too much damned choice.

There are thousands...and thousands...(and many more thousands) of typefaces. And don't even get me started on fonts.

It's like being taken into the largest sweetie shop in the world, where the aisles go on for miles...and miles...in every direction.

Then being asked to choose a favourite sweet.

Just ONE, from amongst everything on offer.

All that mouthwatering selection. All those serifs, san serifs, slabs, hand drawns, scripts...and on...and on...and on...

It would drive me nuts.

So instead, I go for a face that's simple...easy to read...and beautiful. No matter how popular, or how hated, it is.

That's why I'm an unapologetic Helvetica fan.

I'm not a typographer.
I'm an appreciator.
My creativity lies elsewhere.
In writing.

I have always seen beauty in words, sentences, and paragraphs.

But...I have also learned to recognise and appreciate beauty in faces, fonts, and point sizes.

Neon signs, word of mouth, and nailing my feet to the floor.

In the beginning I used to think that writing was a solitary profession.

I was young, stupid, and knew bugger all.

Now I've grown older, I realise I'm still stupid, but at least I know that writing isn't the solitary profession I used to think it was. Well...not all of the time.

It's only that way for some of the time.

We'll call that Part One.

For the rest of the time, it's full of other people.

We'll call that Part Two.

Part One is where you're locked away, on your Jack Jones, with a giant, neon 'do not bloody disturb' sign hanging over the door.

This is the part where your children might forget who you are, and your partner might forget where you are.

Even your pet might think you've abandoned it.

Then there's Part Two.

That's the part where, even if you don't have an agent or a publisher, you're still surrounded by the best support and marketing system in the known universe.

This also applies if you're a copywriter, by the way.

It's called word of mouth.

If you write copy (as I do), this is the part where everyone (art directors, creative directors, other copywriters, account handlers, clients, readers, juniors, cleaners) has an opinion about your words.

All those opinions are valid.

Some of them will flatter your ego.

Some of them will cause you to change and improve your copy.

Some of them will prompt you to tear your hair out.

Some of them will lead you to tearing other folks' hair out.

Suck it up.

They're on your side. Well...most of them.

If you write books (as I do), this is the part where everyone who knows and likes you, spreads the word about your wonderful new missive on every social media site they can think of.

And often you don't even have to ask them. They just do it. Because they want to see you succeed. Because they want to see your book succeed.

They are the literary equivalent of gold dust.

Treat them well. Buy them wine. They are the main reason why your books will sell. Not you.

The trouble is, you become so obsessed with promoting your new book that you stay awake at night, thinking of all the people on the planet who don't know about it.

Then you begin to wonder if there are people on the planet (apart from a select few) who DO know about it.

So you keep on spreading the word.

Once a week.

Sometimes once a day.

Sometimes more.

Then you overhear someone mentioning your name. Then you overhear someone mentioning your writing.

That's when you need people who know how to nod in all the right places...smile at all the right times...and then quickly nail your feet to the floor.

Just to keep you grounded.

Just to keep your head from going anywhere near floating clouds and flying aircraft.

Happily, I have a small group of extremely good friends who are very skilled when it comes to threatening me with a claw hammer and six-inch nails.

They protect me from Cranium Expansion Syndrome.

They remind me that one part of writing involves just me. And the other part involves everyone else.

Readers...editors...proof readers...cover designers...typographers...agents (if necessary)...publishers (again, if necessary)...bloggers...fans...critics...friends...family.

The list goes on...and on.

And they all get ready to do their thing the moment I come out of my locked room and switch off my neon 'do not bloody disturb' sign.

That's when they know I've finished what some would say is the easy part of the book.

Writing the damned thing...

BBH, Robert Carlyle, and The Man Who Walked Around The World.

As anybody who knows me knows...I'm not a whisky fan.
Well...not generally.
And I'm definitely not a Johnnie Walker fan.
My father was.
Maybe that explains a lot.
But I'm definitely a Bartle Bogle Hegarty fan.
And a Robert Carlyle fan.
So I guess you could say I knew them all very well.
But until recently, I didn't know that three of them, Walker, BBH, and Carlyle, came together, in 2009, to produce a stunning PR film that turned into a YouTube sensation...that won a Cannes Lions Gold.
It was called The Man Who Walked Around The World.
It cost less than £100,000 to make. (42)
Peanuts, really.
It squeezed 200 years of Johnnie Walker history into a superbly acted monologue lasting five and a half minutes.
Carlyle did it in one continuous take.
He was brilliant.
But then, so was the script.
Written by Justin Moore ten years after he joined BBH as a junior copywriter in 1999. Before he rose to become Creative Director and then Partner.
Robert Carlyle comes from Maryhill in Glasgow.
As did my father. Coincidentally.

Carlyle is perhaps Scotland's finest actor of his generation. And many other generations.

Moore went on to become Creative Director at Venables Bell and Partners in San Francisco.

Johnnie Walker is the most widely distributed brand of blended Scotch whisky in the world.

Every time I think of Robert Carlyle, I think of Trainspotting.

Don't we all.

Every time I think of legendary copywriters, I think of people like David Abbott, Dave Trott, Susie Henry, David Ogilvy...and John Hegarty, founding partner of BBH.

Again...don't we all.

Every time I think of great pieces of copy, I think of lots of examples. And now there's a new one on my list.

The one written by Justin Moore.

About a man who walked around the world.

It, amongst other examples, should be required listening (and watching, and reading) for every junior copywriter.

So they can realise that great advertising and great storytelling are joined at the bloody hip.

And always should be...

The secret life of my little black books.

Roughly two feet away from my head, to the right of my two pillows, four feet away from the inside of my bedroom door, sits a little black book.

Its close companion is a uni-ball eye fine nib pen. Black ink.

It's the latest in a long line of little black books that I have.

In common with all the others, it has a secret life.

A highly classified existence.

Its right hand pages are recorders of vagrant thoughts and ideas. Interesting words and phrases. Great ideas and fascinating concepts.

For my eyes only.

Those pages go wherever my body goes during the day.

Its left hand pages are recorders of dreams and sleepless reflections. Thoughts I have that keep me awake (or wake me up) during the night.

Thoughts that would disappear like smoke in the wind, were it not for my habit of reaching, bleary eyed, for my little black book. And my uni-ball pen.

Thoughts, again...for my eyes only.

Those pages go wherever my mind goes during the night.

Sometimes the right and left pages meet on neutral ground. Intermingle. Cohabitate. Exchange musings. Occasionally giggle.

They're rebels. Anarchists.

They like breaking rules.

They know no fear.

They love overstepping boundaries. Planting the seeds of a million possibilities. Seeing what pops up.

I'm a freelance copywriter.

Some of my best ideas for ad headlines and body copy have come through the efforts of the right hand pages of my little black book.

I'm an author.

Some of my best ideas for books, short stories, characters, and plots, have come through the efforts of the left hand pages.

There's only one rule that they never break.

In any completed little black book there are no blank pages...except two.

The first page (on the right). And the last page (on the left).

These two pages are kept blank out of respect for the ideas and dreams I'll never have. The headlines and body copy I'll never write. And the characters and plots I'll never create.

They're like the first inch from a newly opened bottle of whisky that's poured over a grave to quench the thirst of the dearly departed.

Never to be tainted by anything as small as minds. Or voices. Or lips. Or words.

If you look at any of my little black books you could be forgiven for thinking that they're just the physical repositories of so much ink on paper.

So much writing during the day.

So much thinking during the night.

But my little black books know better.

They know there's a damned sight more between their covers that you'll never get the chance to see. Or read.

And that's their greatest secret...

Cerebral volume control and The Cocktail Party Effect.

The other week I saw the first episode of a new TV series from the US.

It was a bit sci-fi.

A tad futuristic.

More than a mite interesting.

So I recorded the second episode. And the third.

Anyway...in it, the lead character was a guy who could hear voices in his head.

Thousands of them. All clamouring for attention. All fighting to be heard. They were like rain on his face. He had nowhere to run. Nowhere to hide.

They were driving him nuts.

Then a mysterious stranger taught him how to listen out for one voice amongst all the others.

The one that was saying his name. Over and over.

He listened.

And eventually he heard it.

The stranger taught him how to focus on that one voice.

And ever so slowly, all the other voices dialled down in volume. Slipped into the background.

The rain stopped.

It reminded me of something. I couldn't put my finger on it at first.

Then I remembered an article I'd read about the crazy number of ads (cinema, TV, radio, press, direct mail, posters, neon signs, brand labels, Facebook ads, Google ads, every kind of bloody ad) that Americans are subjected to every day.

The article quoted a figure of somewhere between 4,000 and 10,000. EVERY BLOODY DAY! (43)

And I thought about the TV series about the guy who learned how to tune out the thousands of voices in his head. And a penny dropped.

What if our brains had the ability to dial down all those ads. All that noise. And only let us see the ones that are waving at us. Hear the ones that are calling our name.

Not the ones that we aren't interested in. Not the ones that have nothing to do with us.

What if we didn't have to fight our way through a sea of ideas? All coming right at us.

All clamouring for attention. All fighting to be heard. All driving us nuts.

What if we had our very own cerebral volume control?
Well...we have.

It's called The Cocktail Party Effect. (44)

We use it to block all the sounds we don't want to hear.

We use it to turn down the bad stuff and turn up the good stuff.

They used to call it selective deafness back in the day.

Some folk even think there might be a Cocktail Party Effect for the eyes. A sort of ocular dimmer switch.

Turning down the visibility for all the ads we don't want to see. Turning it up for just the ones we do.

They used to call it selective blindness back in the day.

I've seen a few motorists and pedestrians who suffer from it...

Karma's a bitch, Kevin.

I read an old article today in The Guardian online.

It was written by Ali Hanan, Creative Director at Creative Equals, and published in February of 2016.

I was catching up.

It was one of those belated moments, for an article of hers that I didn't catch first time around.

Its title is "Five facts that show how the advertising industry fails women."

You'll find it here: http://bit.ly/2bEm2lB

It was also one of those struck-a-chord moments.

I wondered if it was just as true now (15 months later) as it was when it was written.

Here's why...

For as long as I've been in the business (a mere 35 years, give or take), I've never been able to figure out why ad agencies don't have more female Creative Directors.

It's not as if the talent's not there. It is.

It's not as if the talent's not good enough. It definitely is.

It's not as if the talent's not willing enough. It absolutely is.

Sadly, my experience of just how male-dominated the industry has been since, well...forever, is embarrassingly one-sided.

The side that wears boxer shorts tends to predominate.

I remember reading about a senior 'mad man' who firmly believed that gender equality in advertising was dead in the water. Wasn't even worth talking about.

Read my lips.

Bollocks...

What I can't for the life of me understand is this, and I quote:

"Females make up 85% of all purchasing decisions, yet are woefully underrepresented in creative jobs in advertising."

How the hell is that possible?

Pause for breath.

Now...remember those five facts I mentioned earlier? Here they are. Please note, they're just a year old.

One: 88% of young, female creatives say they lack role models.

Two: 70% of young female creatives say they have never worked with a female creative director or executive creative director.

Three: 70% of young female creatives are working in a 75% male-dominated department.

Four: 60% of young females say they believe advertising is a career that doesn't support young families.

Five: 10% of young male creatives are working in an all-make department.

Pause for thought.

As I've said many times...a great idea doesn't care who it happens to. Doesn't care what age, colour, height, weight, or creed you are. And it sure as hell doesn't care what sex you are.

You don't need to be testosterone-bloody-friendly to be a great copywriter, art director, or creative director.

Google the following:

Helen Lansdowne Resor...Christine Frederick...Mathilde C. Weil...Charlotte Beers...Helen Gurley Brown...Jane Mass...Kat Gordon...Susie Henry...Lisa Leone...Christine Call...Brandy Cole...Lena Kuffner...Marissa Shrum...Julia Neumann...and, yes, Ali Hanan.

The list goes on...and on...

It's not like the role models aren't out there. They bloody well are.

So what's the problem, people?

In the September 10, 2014 edition of Adweek, an article by the late, great, Noreen O'Leary carried the headline: "Women are now winning 11% of Creative Director Awards, up from 4% in 2004."

This iconic giant of advertising journalism sadly passed away aged 59, in 2016. But for 31 years, O'Leary set the standard for covering the ad world. She is sorely missed.

In another article, this time published in Guardian US in August 2016, reporter Jana Kasperkevic wrote:

"Dozens of women in advertising gathered under the chandeliers of Cipriani's restaurant in midtown Manhattan on Wednesday to celebrate the best in their field, but the celebration was marred by another bitter reminder that the ad industry is still stuck in the Mad Men era of 1960s.

"Just hours before the 2016 Women to Watch luncheon, Kevin Roberts announced that he was resigning from his position as the executive chairman at Saatchi & Saatchi following his remarks that the "debate is all over" on gender equality in the ad industry and that women lack "vertical ambition". (45)

Read my lips.
Karma's a bitch, Kevin...

Ad Lib, Ad Hoc, and throwing balls in the air.

Writing books (or writing anything come to think of it) is a little like throwing balls in the air. There's just no damned fun in just throwing up one.

It's much more fun when you have two, or more writing projects, on the go at the same time. And it's a lot more interesting.

Especially if they come back with more words than they had when they left.

So naturally when I was writing Ad Lib, I began to think about a sequel.

Well...actually I began thinking of a sequel when I realised I was trying to squeeze a quart into a pint pot with Ad Lib, so to speak.

And that's when I began to think about Ad Hoc.

Ad Hoc is the second compilation of articles written by me as a sort of running social media blog. Truth be told, sometimes it runs...sometimes it jogs...and sometimes it sort of ambles along casually, taking in the views.

So if you like Ad Lib, and you're the kind of person who doesn't see the point of just having one tasty mouthful of anything when you can have two (or more)...then have a look out for Ad Hoc.

It should be up on Amazon at the end of 2017 or the beginning of 2018.

It's exactly the same as Ad Lib...only completely different.

References.

PAGE	REFERENCE:
67.	(1). http://bit.ly/2xN1KGv
74.	(2). http://dailym.ai/2x2ATSI
76.	(3). http://bit.ly/1M13Nbt
88.	(4). http://bit.ly/2zv8K8r
103.	(5). http://bit.ly/2gL9j6c
107.	(6). http://bit.ly/2ypdXk9
119.	(7). www.worldometers.info
	(8). www.curious.astro.cornell.edu
132.	(9). http://bit.ly/2lxgH8u
133.	(10). http://bit.ly/1DDXLsl
135.	(11). http://bit.ly/JAtIPY
	(12). http://ti.me/2xNeh7W
	(13). http://read.bi/2xOitcJ
	(14). http://bit.ly/2ySevjt
	(15). http://bit.ly/2ghlLty
	(16). http://bit.ly/2xNkvoI
	(17). http://bit.ly/2hNGINg
	(18). http://bit.ly/2ywvXZ6
138.	(19). http://bbc.in/1N56LKi
149.	(20). http://bit.ly/2hNA2yR
159.	(21). http://bit.ly/2gkXROP
	(22). http://bit.ly/2kjHeF8
	(23). http://bit.ly/2tjHHc7
161.	(24). http://bit.ly/2xN4WgL
170.	(25). http://bit.ly/2gqQI2w
183.	(26). http://bit.ly/1TfVTML
	(27). http://bit.ly/2h8hZkK
203.	(28). http://es.pn/2yRR4qe
226.	(29). http://bit.ly/2yRlRng
235.	(30). http://bit.ly/2yxS4Po
244.	(31). http://bbc.in/2luKfUb

	(32). http://bit.ly/2gNR6Fc
248.	(33). http://bit.ly/2kYWFVx
252.	(34). http://bit.ly/2qshwRQ
253.	(35). http://bit.ly/2zi0iZc
282.	(36). http://bit.ly/2ywZ66z
283.	(37). http://bit.ly/2xNZnOV
284.	(38). http://bit.ly/1qe3M4Y
	(39). http://bit.ly/2kYridL
288.	(40). http://nyti.ms/2x5E8Ze
290.	(41). http://bit.ly/2zydc63
299.	(42). http://bit.ly/2gOuwwb
304.	(43). http://bit.ly/2c3Jo7f
	(44). http://bit.ly/2gODZTU
307.	(45). http://bit.ly/2imKlh6

www.ingramcontent.com/pod-product-compliance
Lightning Source LLC
Chambersburg PA
CBHW050048230526
45470CB00004B/1450